ABANDONED VICTORIA

GHOSTS OF THE GARDEN STATE

SHANE THOMS

AUSTRALIA THROUGH TIME

The creators of this book's content fully acknowledge and recognise the Traditional Custodians of the land on which these structures were built and pay our respects to all elders past, present, and emerging. Although this publication does not deeply explore the Indigenous stories of the spaces explored, the creators of its content recognise that Australia's First Nations people have occupied and cared for this continent for over 65,000 years. And no matter where we are across this nation, Australia always was and always will be Aboriginal and Torres Strait Islander land.

With thanks to Sayaka Treeve and Heidi Eager

Australia Through Time
is an imprint jointly owned by

Woodslane Press Pty Ltd, 10 Apollo Street, Warriewood, NSW 2102, Australia
Email: info@woodslane.com.au
Tel: 02 8445 2300
Website: woodslanepress.com.au

and

Fonthill Media, Millview, Toadsmoor Road, Stroud, GL5 2TB, United Kingdom
Tel: 01453 886959
Website: www.fonthill.media

First published in Australia in 2025 by Fonthill Media and Woodslane Press

NATIONAL LIBRARY OF AUSTRALIA

A catalogue record for this book is available from the National Library of Australia

MIX
Paper | Supporting responsible forestry
FSC www.fsc.org FSC® C006474

Printed in China by SC (Sang Choy) International Pte Ltd

WOODSLANE PRESS

FONTHILL

CONTENTS

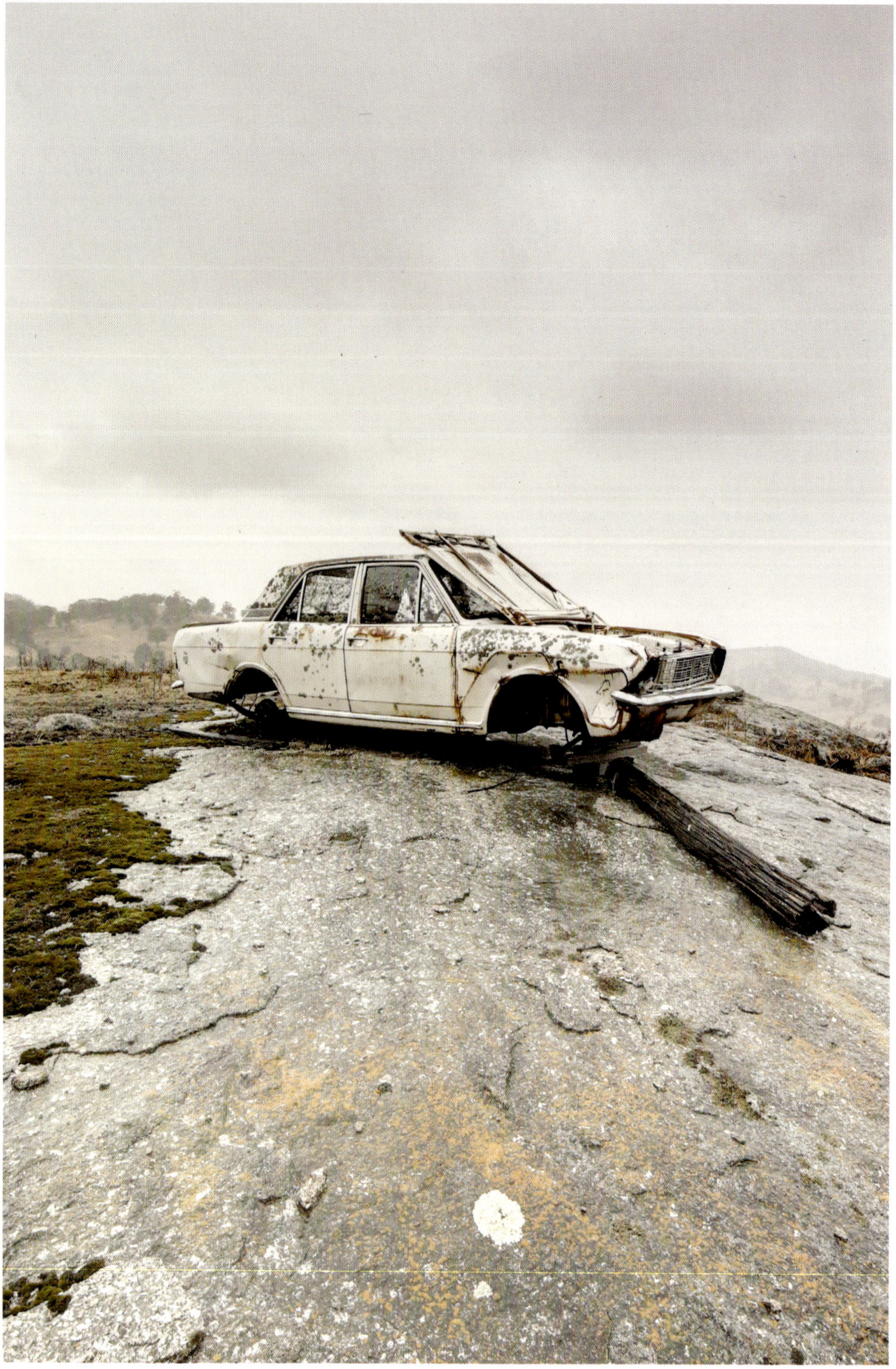
A rusting car wreck teeters on the edge of a cliff in Victoria's remote High Country.

INTRODUCTION

The abandoned places scattered across Victoria tell a story of change, ambition and adaptation. From gold rush towns that flourished and faded, to derelict industrial sites, these locations offer a tangible connection to the state's past, its economic booms and busts, its shifting industries and the evolving urban landscapes that have shaped Victoria over time.

The land on which these abandoned post-colonial spaces stand has for tens of thousands of years been home to the Wurundjeri, Bunurong, Dja Dja Wurrung and other Aboriginal peoples, who have maintained enduring cultural and spiritual connections to these regions. Today, these sites—and the waterways that run through them—remain deeply significant, continuing to carry the stories, practices and living presence of the region's First Nations communities.

The Victorian gold rush of the 1850s sparked rapid settlement and economic expansion, with towns emerging around rich deposits almost overnight. Places like Walhalla, once a bustling mining hub, now stand as quiet reminders of that era, embodying the fleeting nature of gold-driven prosperity. The rise and fall of these settlements highlight how resource extraction shaped Victoria's development and how quickly fortunes could shift when the gold was gone.

Victoria's abandoned hospitals reflect the shifting landscape of healthcare across the state, with institutions such as the Larundel and Mooroopna facilities standing as stark reminders of once-thriving community care centres. These hospitals were established to serve both urban and rural populations but were gradually closed due to centralisation of health services, funding cuts or outdated infrastructure. As medicine advanced and attitudes toward patient care evolved, smaller or isolated hospitals were often deemed unsustainable. Today, these now eroded structures tell the silent stories of medical histories and the growing pains of a health system in constant transition.

The townships of Victoria, particularly those in the central Latrobe Valley, have witnessed the rise and decline of key industries over time. Towering among these legacies are the region's decommissioned power stations, once vital to the state's electricity supply. For decades, these facilities shaped the economic and social fabric of the valley, employing thousands and fuelling Victoria's industrial growth. As energy production has shifted toward renewable sources, these power stations have been shuttered, leaving behind vast, silent structures. Today, what remains serves as a monument to a pivotal era in the state's history and a reminder of the complex shift from coal-based industry to cleaner, more sustainable energy.

When discussing the state's thriving capital, it's impossible to ignore the role of street art in shaping Melbourne's identity, particularly within its abandoned spaces. In recent decades, many of Victoria's forgotten interiors, such as Larundel Asylum, Box Hill Brickworks, Geelong Power Station and the Bradmill denim factory, have served as unofficial studios for emerging and established artists alike. These neglected sites have provided a raw, unregulated environment in which artists can experiment freely, hone their skills and develop the distinctive, expressive style that now characterises Melbourne's urban art scene. Rather than traditional galleries or formal training spaces, these dilapidated buildings have nurtured creativity through their very decay—offering walls, floors and surfaces as blank canvases for practice, play and personal expression. It's in these derelict structures that many artists first pushed boundaries, tested ideas and formed visual identities away from the public eye. Far from being merely sites of ruin, these places have become incubators for artistic growth, where spray paint, thought and space converge to shape the next wave of Melbourne's creative voices.

Contemporary commentary on Victoria wouldn't be complete without an analysis of the region's escalating housing problem—driven by rapid population growth and a severe shortage of affordable homes that stand in stark contrast to the presence of abandoned houses dotted around the state. Located in both rural areas and inner-city suburbs, this situation highlights a profound disconnect between existing, unused dwellings and the urgent need to house a fast-growing population.

Together, these forgotten places, whether relics of boomtowns, closed hospitals, shuttered industries, or empty homes, reveal the complexities of Victoria's past and present, inviting us to reflect not only on what has been left behind, but on what kind of future we choose to build in their shadows. They also prompt a deeper question: what purpose do these spaces serve us now? As sites of memory, exploration, creativity and contemplation, they continue to shape how we engage with history, identity and the evolving story of place.

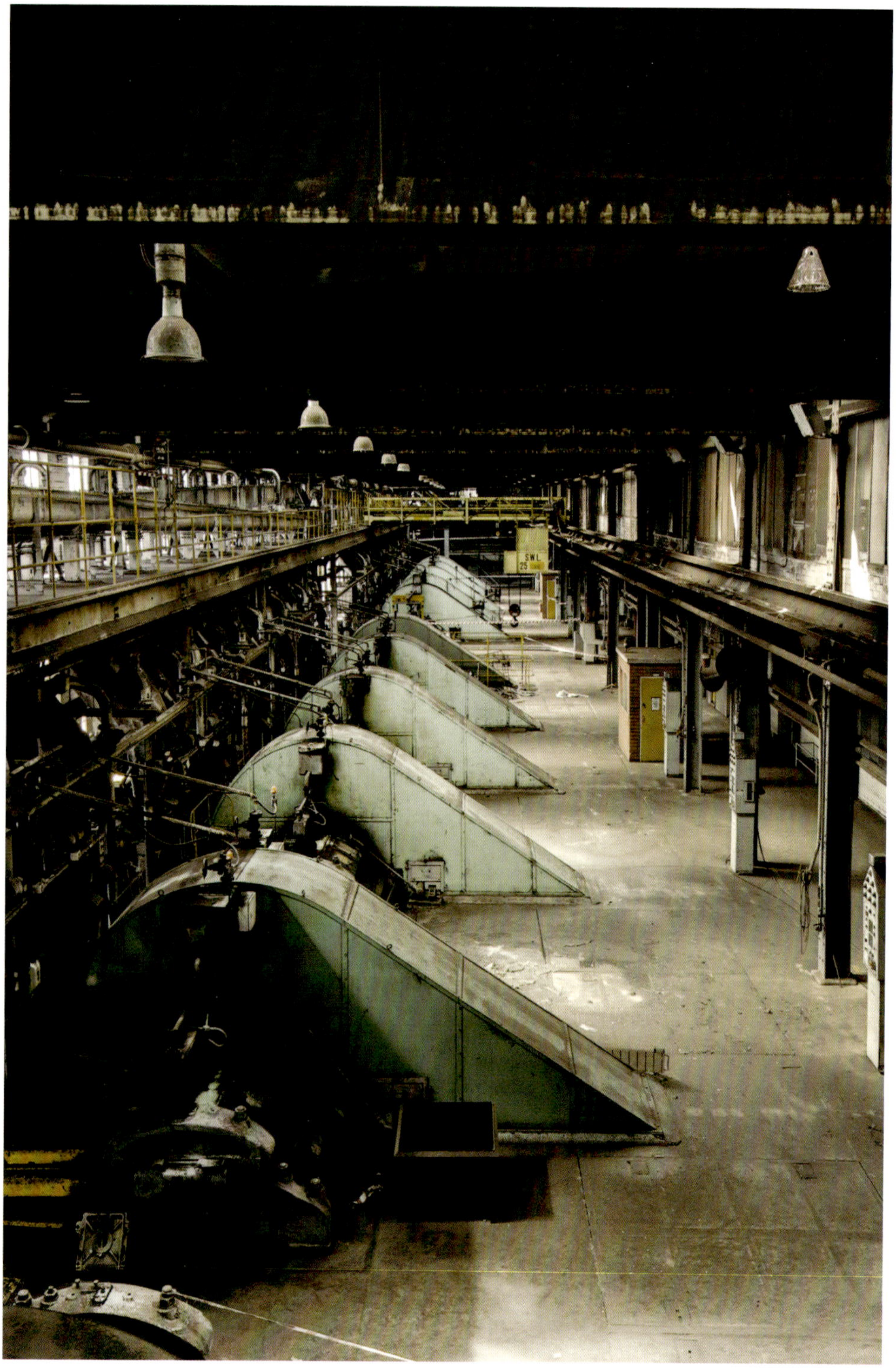

Heavy industrial relics line the floor, untouched since the power plant fell silent.

THE POWER STATION

Located in the central Victorian township of Morwell, this vast power station was a cornerstone of Australia's energy infrastructure throughout much of the 20th century. Constructed between 1949 and 1956, it played a vital role in supplying electricity for both industrial and residential purposes and was intrinsically linked to the economic development and social identity of the Latrobe Valley.

The plant was one of several coal-fired power stations in the region, an area rich in brown coal reserves. The power station not only supplied electricity to Victoria's grid but was also essential in producing briquettes—compact blocks of dried brown coal—for home heating and industrial fuel. At its peak, the complex employed hundreds of workers, contributing to the region's identity as Victoria's power-producing heartland.

For decades, the power station provided stable employment and supported local communities, reinforcing the Latrobe Valley's role as an energy hub. The briquette industry was particularly vital in post-war Australia, helping to meet the country's growing energy demands. The station's operation also contributed to technological advancements in coal processing and energy production.

With increasing environmental concerns and the transition toward cleaner energy sources, the power plant, like other coal-fired facilities, faced growing challenges. By the early 2000s, demand for brown coal briquettes had declined significantly. The power station officially closed in 2014, marking the end of an era for the Latrobe Valley's coal industry.

The closure of the plant left economic and environmental concerns in its wake. The loss of jobs was a significant blow to the region, highlighting the broader challenges of transitioning from coal to renewable energy.

The power station was a pillar of Victoria's energy supply and a defining feature of the Latrobe Valley's economy. While its closure marked a shift in Australia's energy landscape, it also underscored the complexities of balancing economic stability with environmental sustainability. Today, the site is a reminder of the region's industrial heritage and the ongoing transition toward cleaner energy solutions.

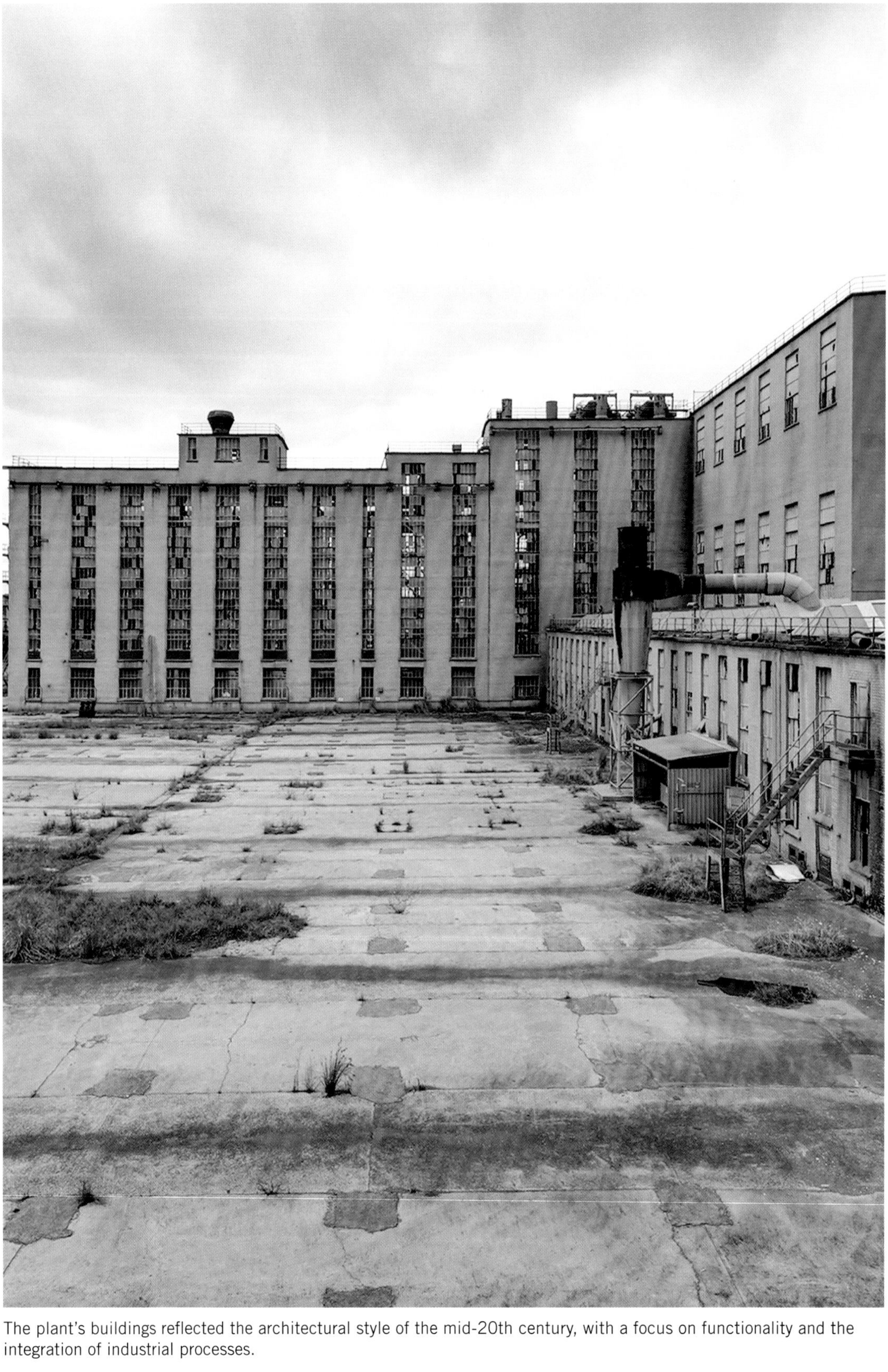

The plant's buildings reflected the architectural style of the mid-20th century, with a focus on functionality and the integration of industrial processes.

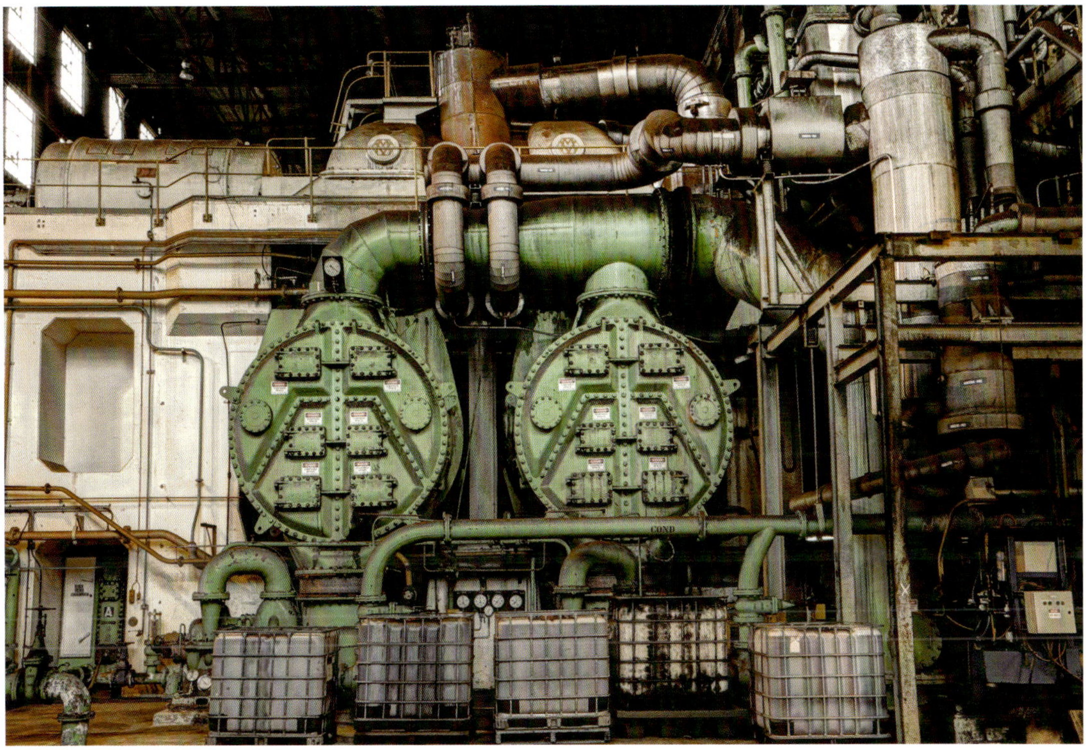

Deep within the power plant, complex machinery orchestrates a vast network of interwoven pipes.

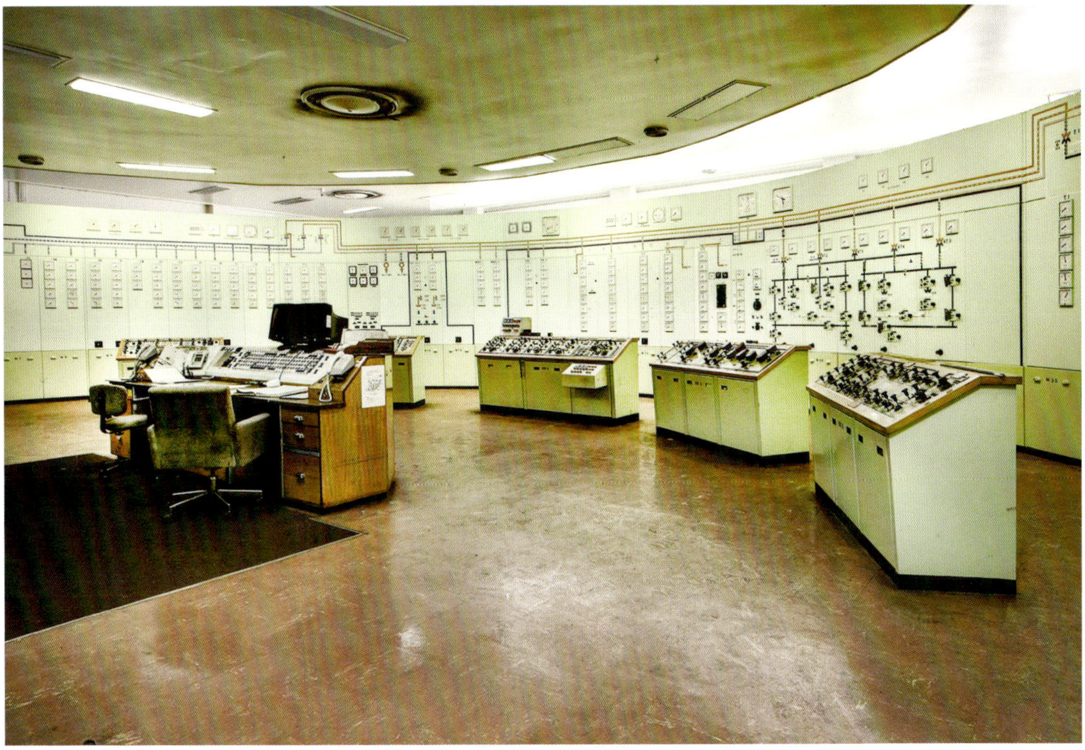

Bathed in retro lime green, this control room feels like it belongs in a classic Bond movie—one of many scattered throughout the plant.

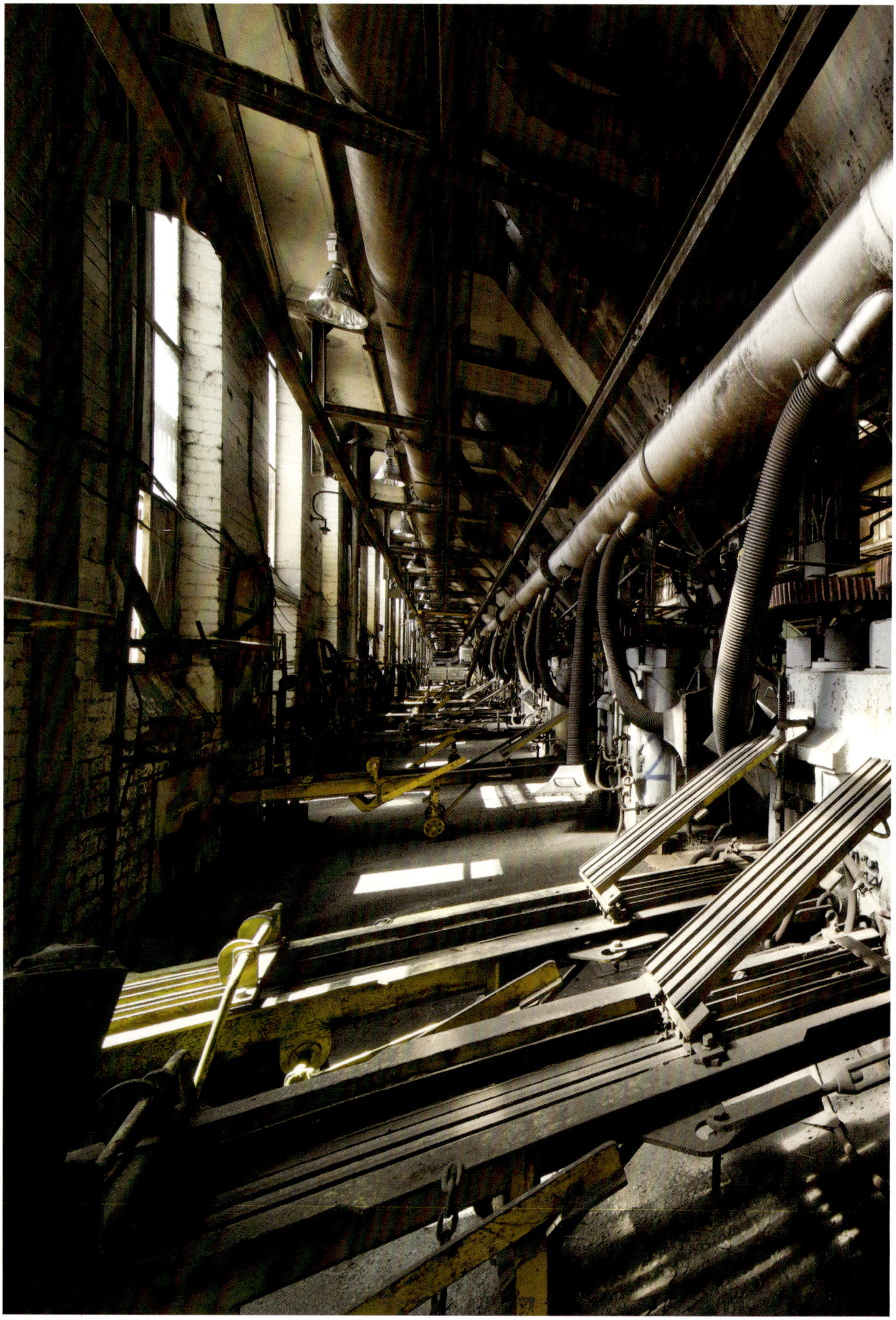

Endless rows of silent machines disappear into the shadows.

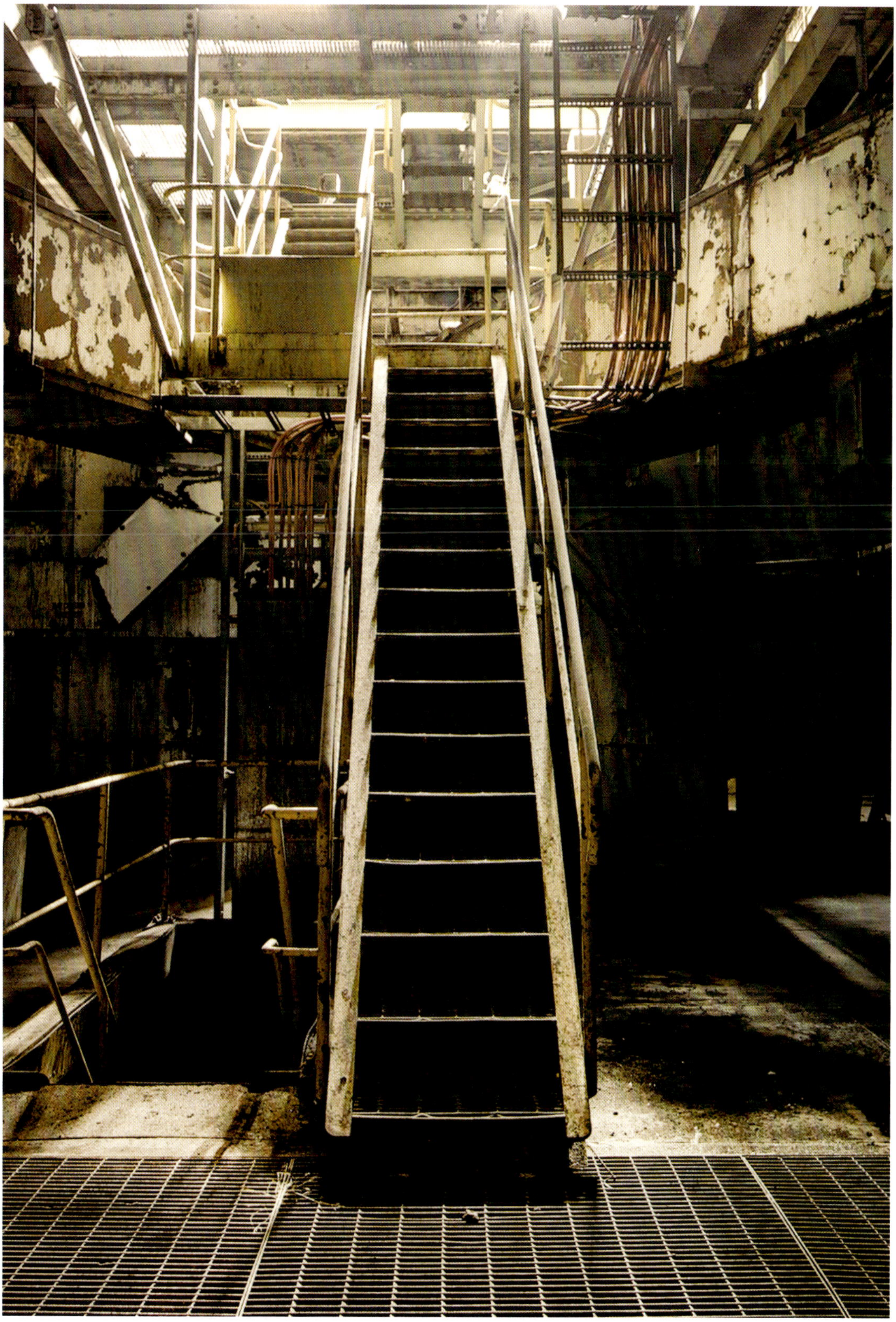

A narrow stairway descends into darkness, leading deeper into the factory's forgotten core.

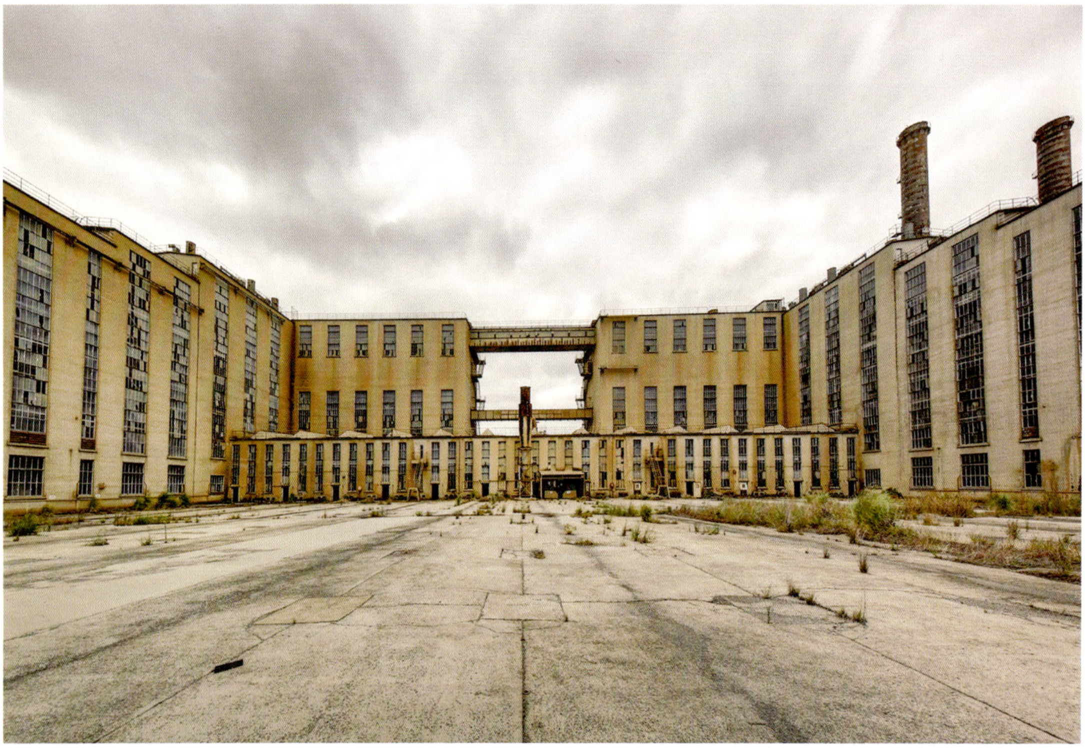

Brutal and utilitarian, the functional architecture of Morwell's Energy Brix Power Plant reflects an era when form bowed to industry and efficiency.

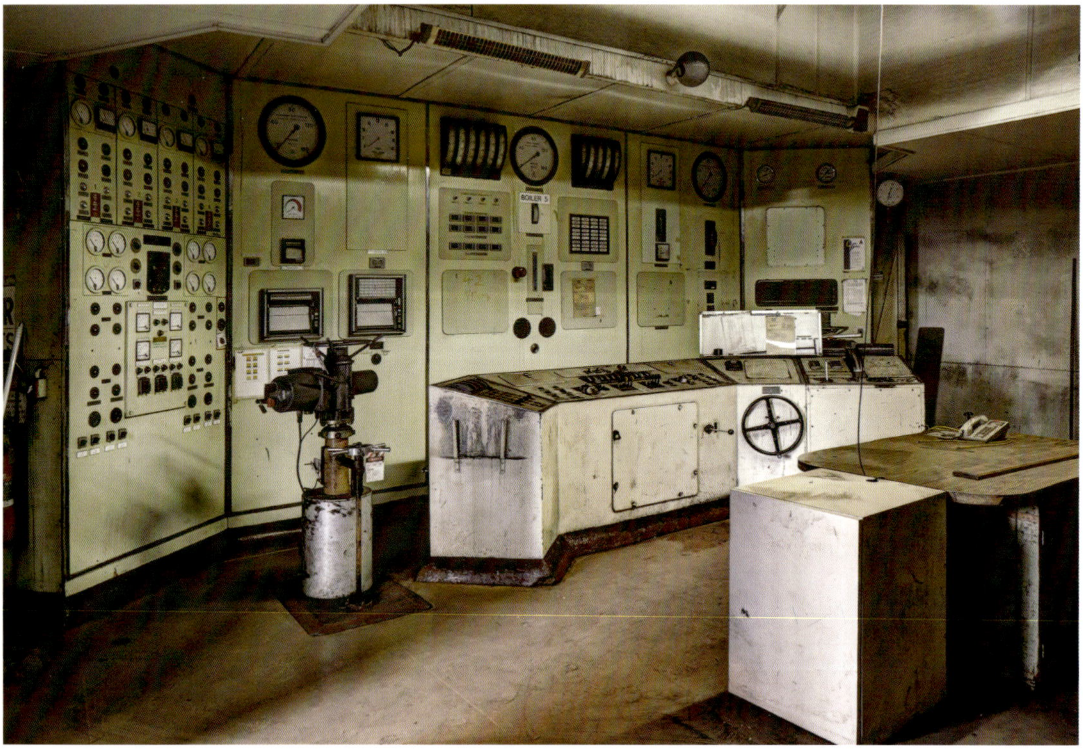

Shrouded in darkness at the heart of the power station, this grimy control room is now tended only by silence and dust.

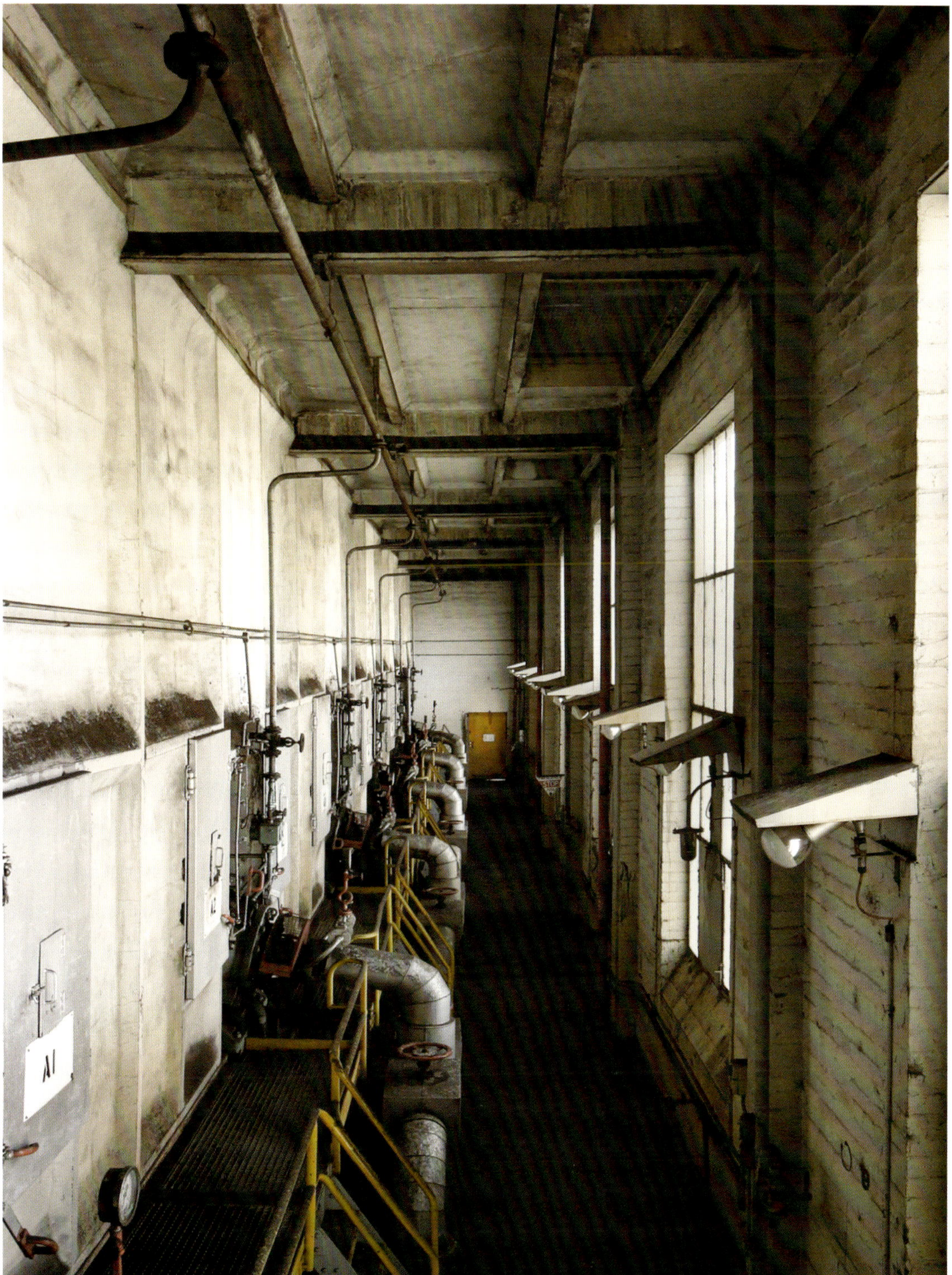

A row of heavy pipes snakes downward along the factory floor, like arteries in an industrial corpse.

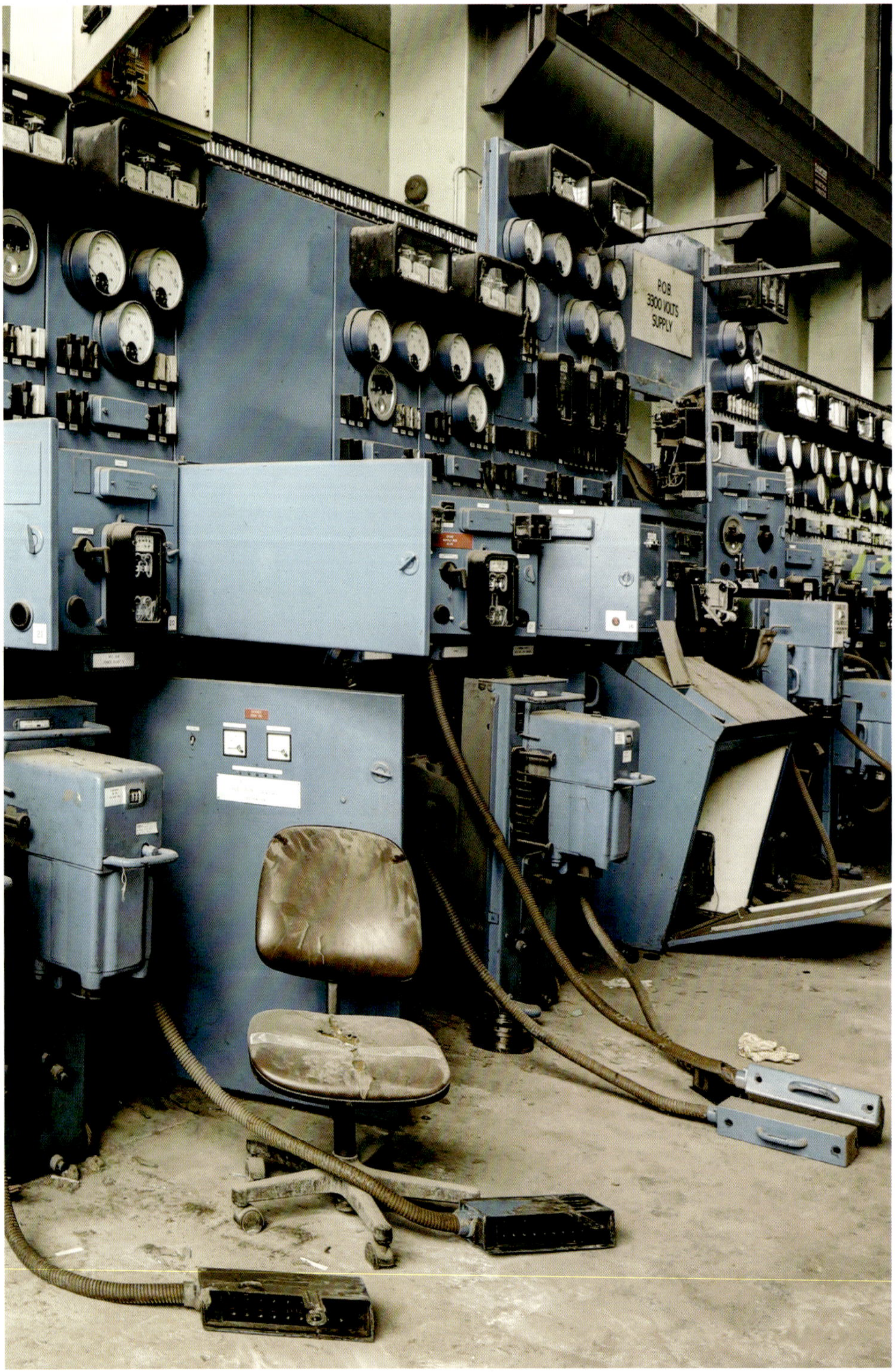

The blue control room of the Fairfield Paper Mill—now demolished—its vintage dials, switches and lights once buzzed with activity.

THE PAPER MILL

The former Fairfield Paper Mill, on the banks of the Yarra River in Melbourne, played a strong role in Victoria's industrial development. Established in the early 1900s, the mill was part of Australia's growing paper manufacturing industry, supplying newsprint and packaging materials to support the country's expanding economy.

The Mill contributed significantly to local employment, drawing workers from the surrounding suburbs and helping to establish Fairfield as an industrial hub with the nearby Yarra River providing essential water resources for paper production. By the late 20th century, shifts in manufacturing and environmental concerns led to the decline of the mill. It was eventually closed and later demolished, making way for a housing development. Despite its disappearance, the Fairfield Paper Mill remains an important part of Melbourne's industrial heritage, reflecting the city's transition from heavy industry to a more urban landscape.

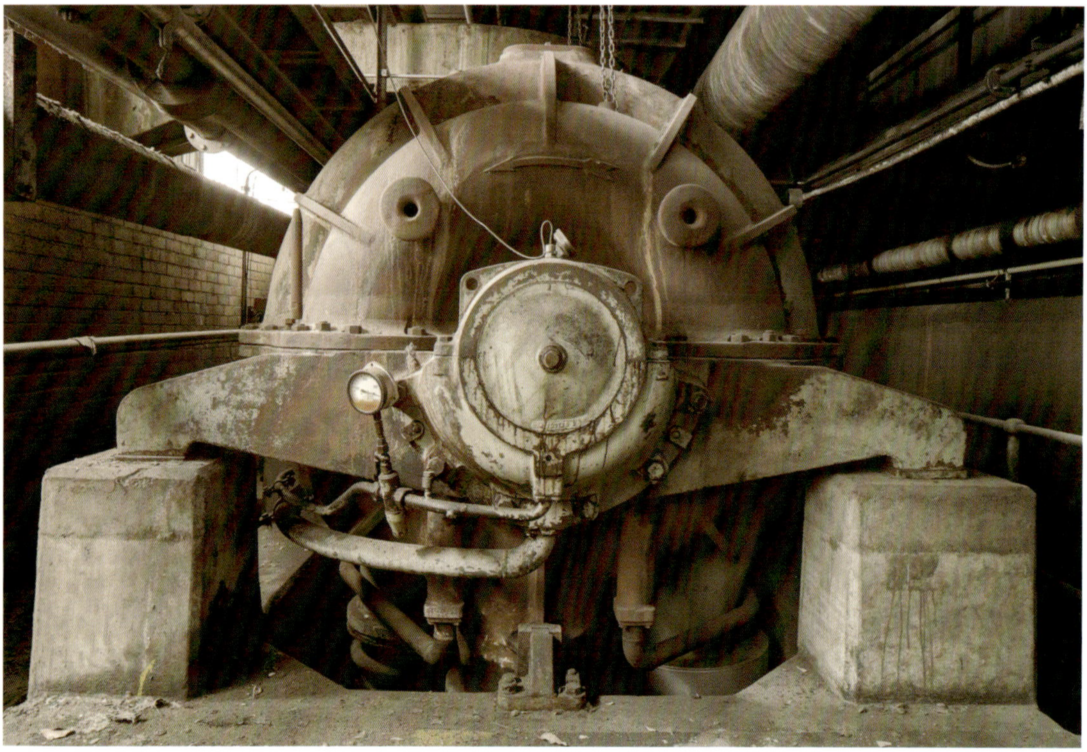

Buried in the depths of the paper mill, a wide, circular machine sits like a forgotten sentinel.

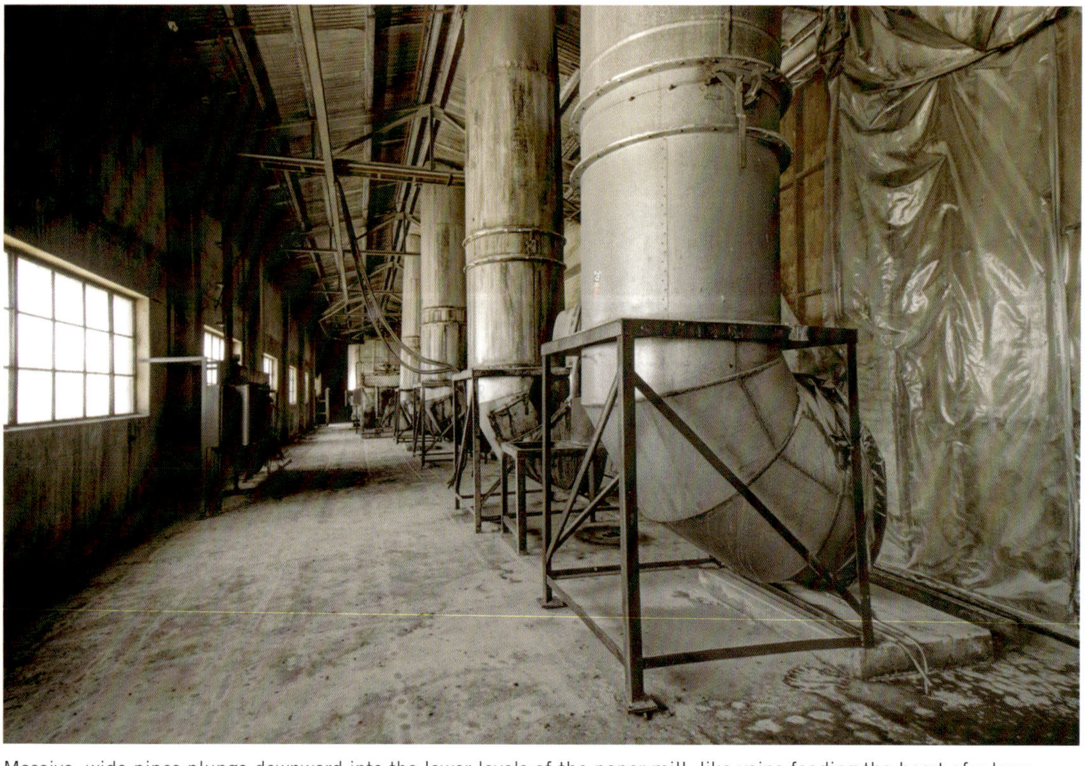

Massive, wide pipes plunge downward into the lower levels of the paper mill, like veins feeding the heart of a long-silent machine.

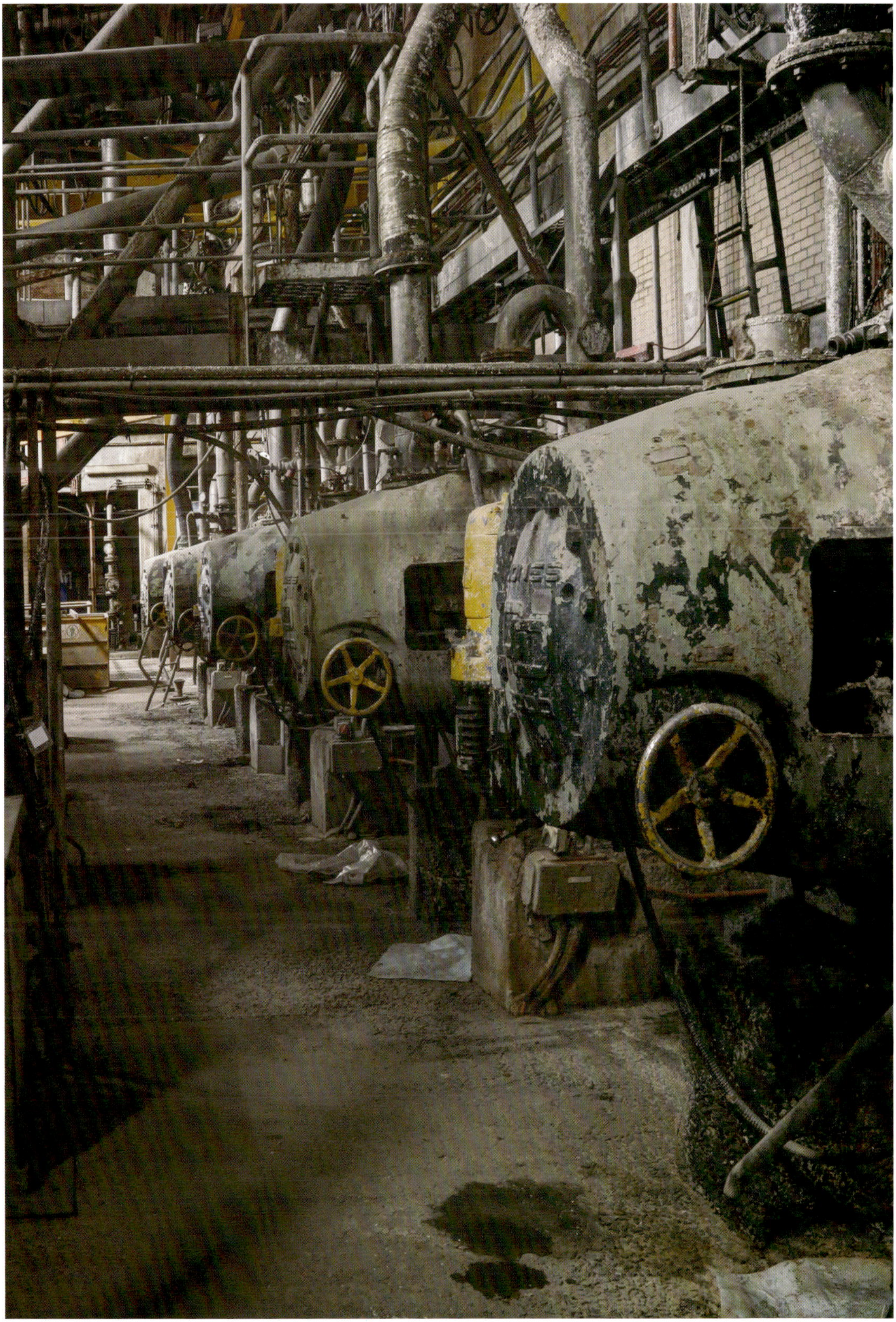

Once integral to the creation of paper and packaging, this line of grime-caked machinery now rests discarded on the industrial scrap heap—silent relics of a production line long shut down.

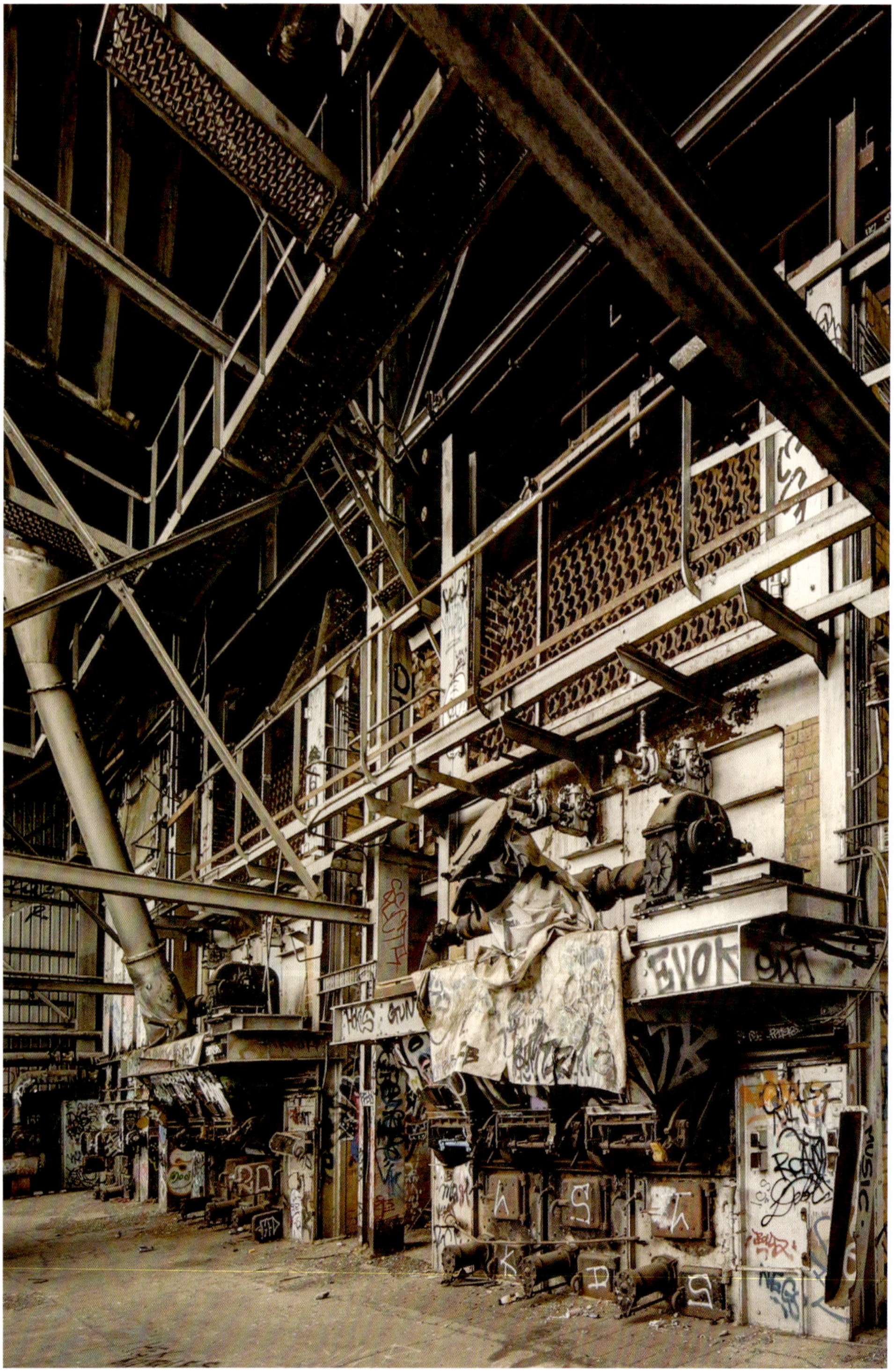

Rusted and forgotten, this machinery sits in silence—ghostly reminders of a factory that once echoed with the labour of hundreds of Melbourne workers.

THE DENIM FACTORY

The Bradmill Factory in Melbourne, once a thriving textile manufacturing hub, now stands as a decaying relic of Victoria's industrial past. Located in Yarraville, the factory played a crucial role in the state's economy, providing employment for generations of workers and contributing to Australia's once-booming textile industry. Its closure reflects the broader decline of manufacturing in Victoria, the impact of globalisation and the shift towards offshore production. Today, the abandoned site serves as a reminder of both the prosperity it once brought to the community and the economic shifts that led to its demise.

Established in the 1920s, Bradmill was one of Australia's leading textile manufacturers, specializing in denim production. The factory supplied material for workwear, school uniforms and denim clothing at a time when local manufacturing was essential for Australia's post-World War II economy. At its peak, Bradmill employed hundreds of workers, many of whom lived in the surrounding western suburbs of Melbourne. It provided stable jobs, fostering a strong working-class community built around industrial labour.

By the late 20th century, Victoria's manufacturing sector faced significant challenges. The rise of cheaper offshore production, coupled with changes in trade policies and economic restructuring, led to the gradual decline of local textile industries. Bradmill, like many other Australian manufacturers, struggled to compete with imported fabrics from countries with lower labour costs. The factory eventually closed in the early 2000s, leaving behind not only an abandoned industrial site but also a workforce that was required to adapt to a changing job market.

Since its closure, the Bradmill Factory has become a well-known discarded site, attracting urban explorers, artists and photographers. Its graffiti-covered walls and crumbling infrastructure stand as a visual representation of industrial decline. Caught between its historical significance and the pressures of urban growth, the area has been approved for a new housing development.

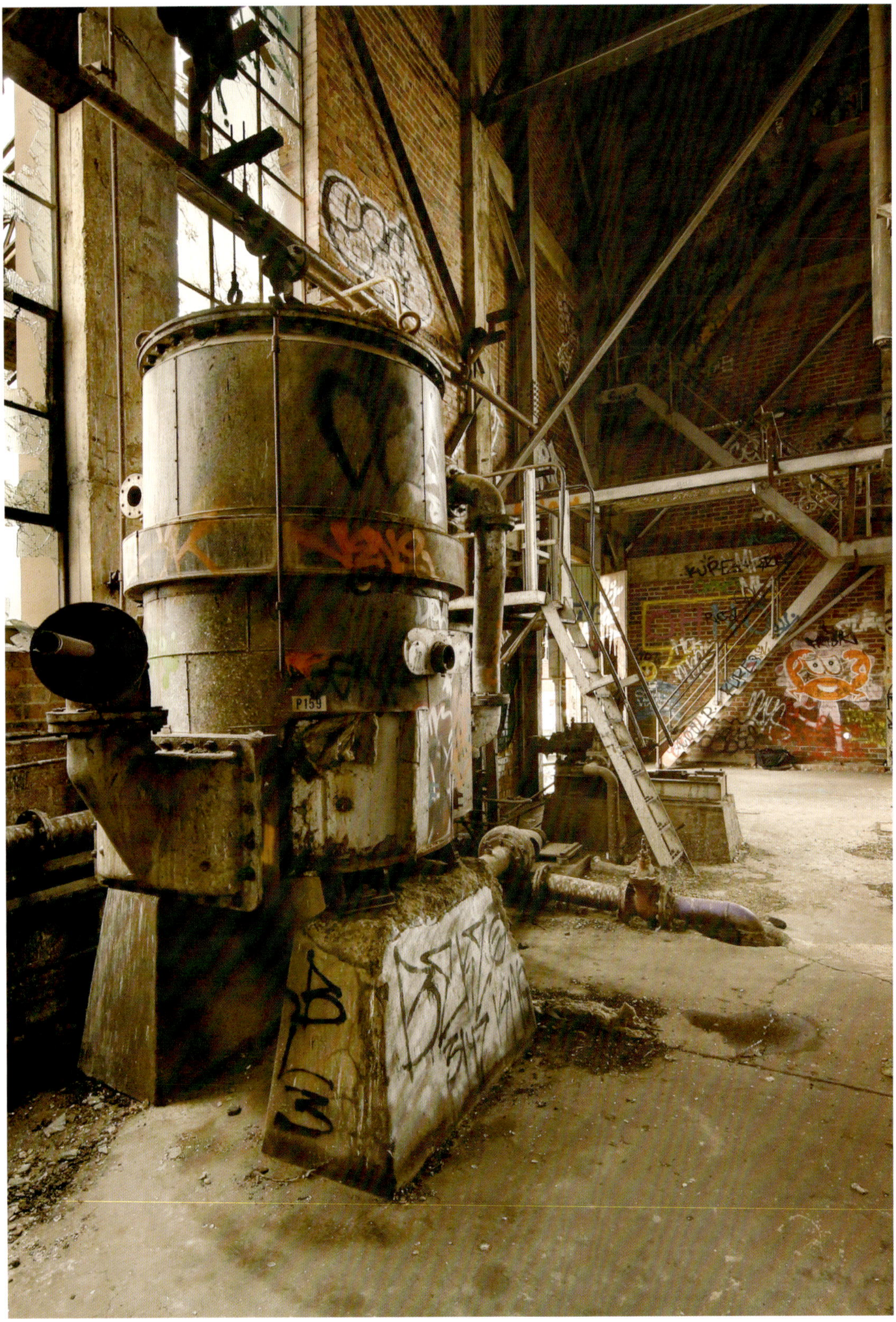

A graffiti-covered boiler stands defaced and defiant in the disused denim factory—its industrial past now cloaked in layers of urban expression.

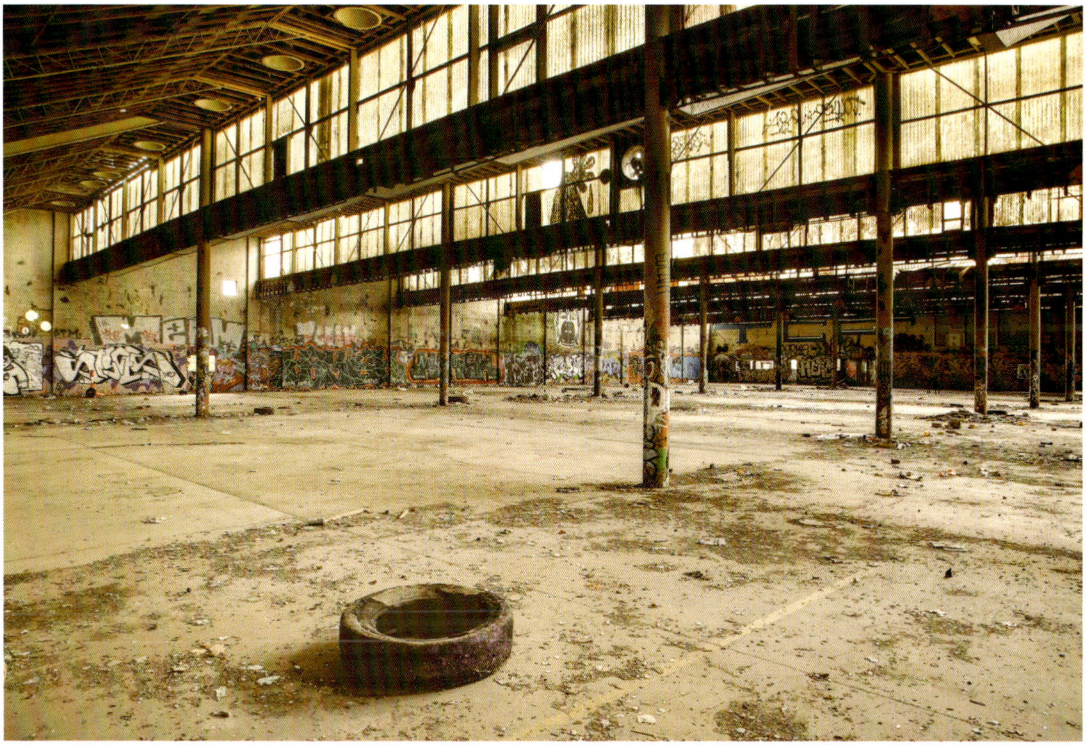

The vast interior of the denim factory, once humming with industry, became a sprawling canvas where graffiti artists claimed the walls with colour and expression.

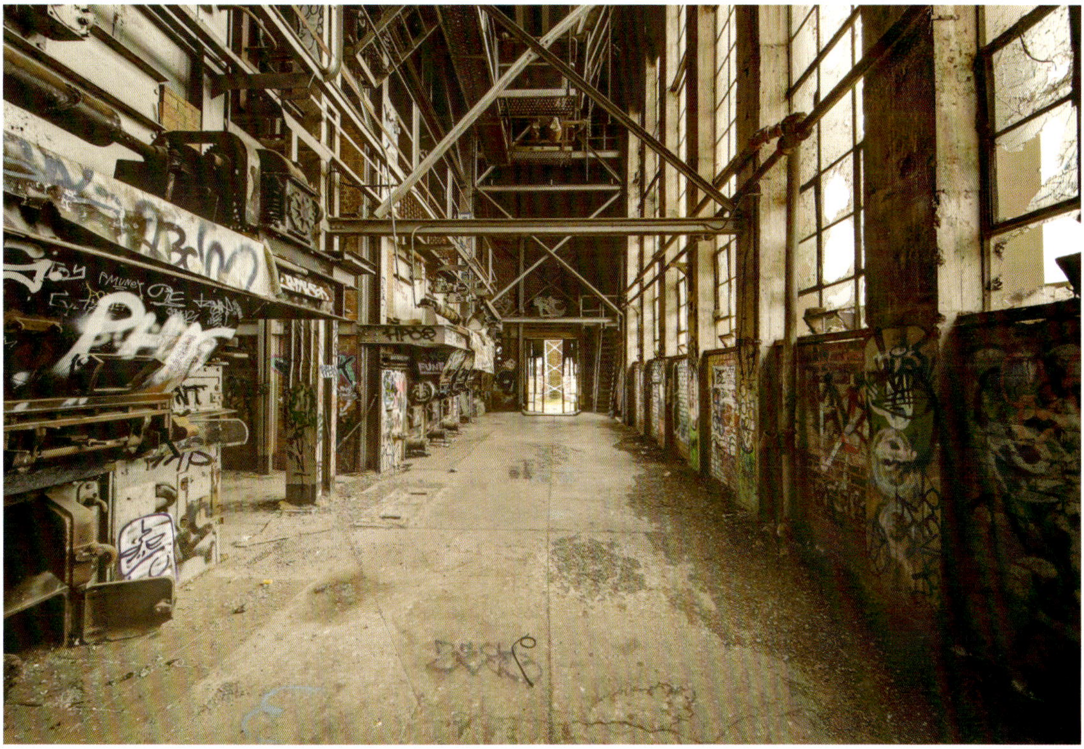

A long view through the denim factory reveals rows of lifeless machinery, suspended in silence, like ghosts of industry still haunting the space they once served.

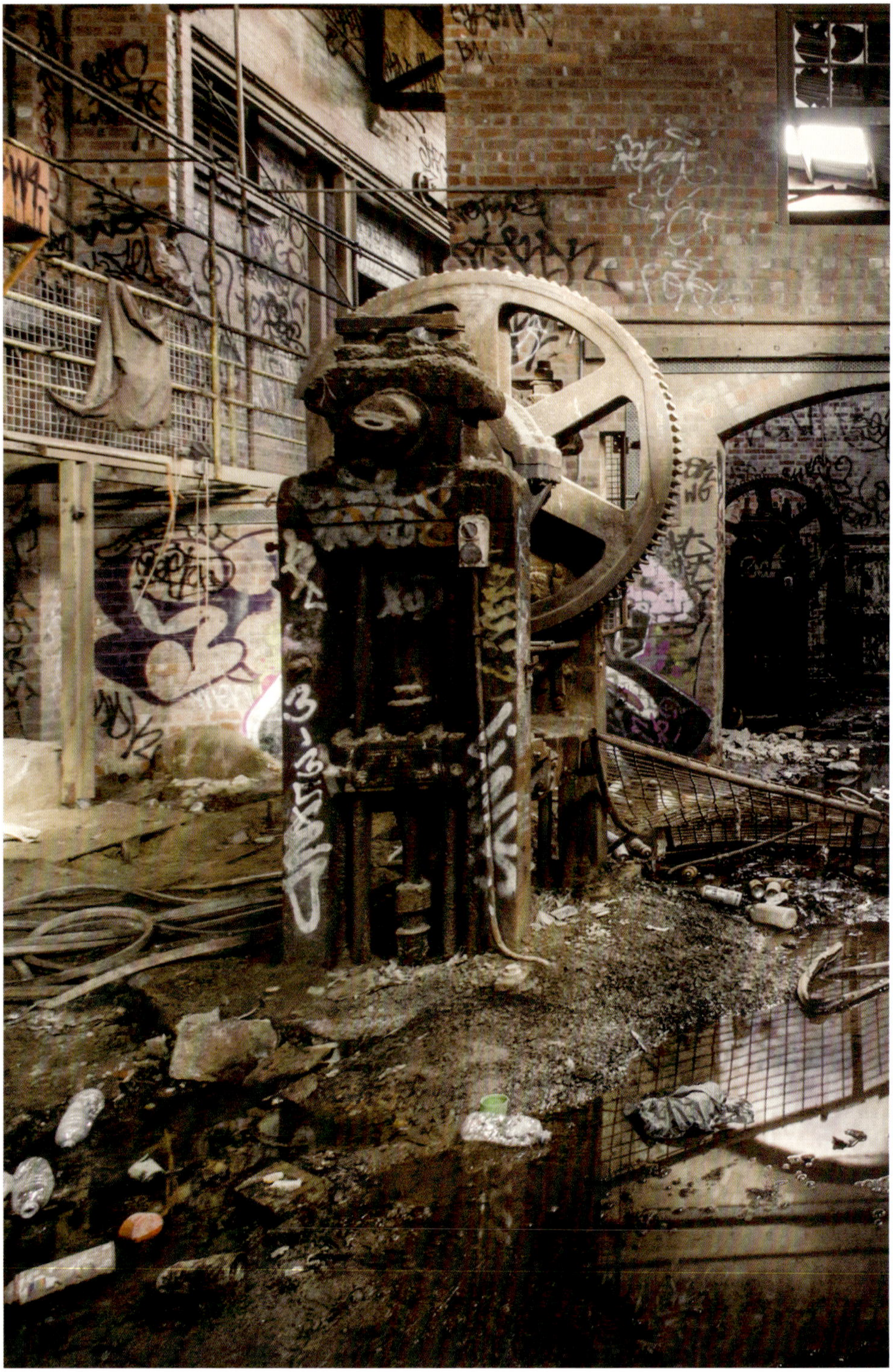

Gigantic rusted cogs loom in the long-abandoned Box Hill brick factory. Years of weathering have turned the site into a muddy graveyard of industrial decay.

THE BRICK WORKS

The Box Hill Brickworks, once a key industrial site in Melbourne's eastern suburbs, played a significant role in Victoria's construction industry. Established in the late 19th century, the brickworks supplied materials for Melbourne's rapid urban expansion, producing high-quality bricks used in housing and infrastructure projects.

At its peak, the site featured kilns, chimneys and clay pits, employing many local workers. However, by the mid-late 20th century, demand declined as brickmaking technology evolved, and production shifted elsewhere. The site was eventually abandoned, leaving behind derelict structures that became a hotspot for urban exploration, graffiti and local subcultures.

In the decades that followed its closure, the Brickworks took on a new identity as a creative playground for photographers and artists. Its weathered textures, decaying architecture and industrial remnants provided a compelling visual backdrop for photo shoots and art installations, drawing in creatives intrigued by its haunting beauty and raw aesthetic. The site's layered history and sense of desolation offered fertile ground for artistic interpretation. From stylised portrait sessions to immersive video shoots, the abandoned brickworks became a space where creative expression thrived—its silence and deterioration adding a powerful narrative to every image captured within its walls.

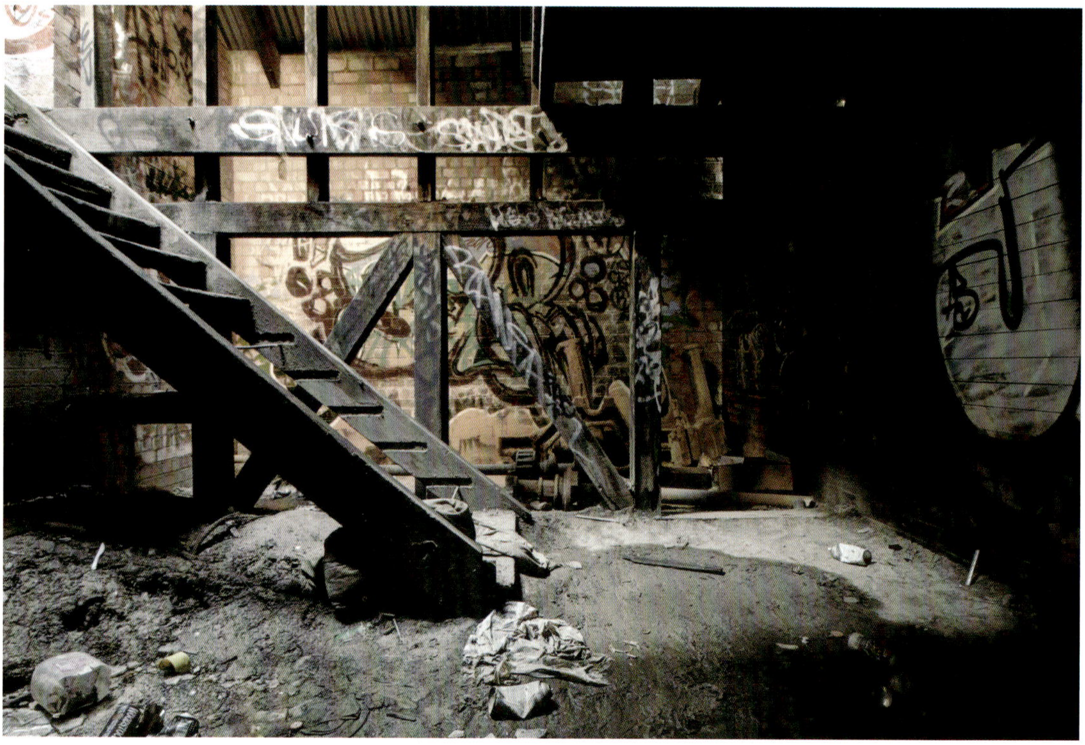

A wooden stairway descends into the lower level—a rare remnant that hints at the factory's age. It's a quiet reminder of craftsmanship in a space largely surrendered to rot and ruin.

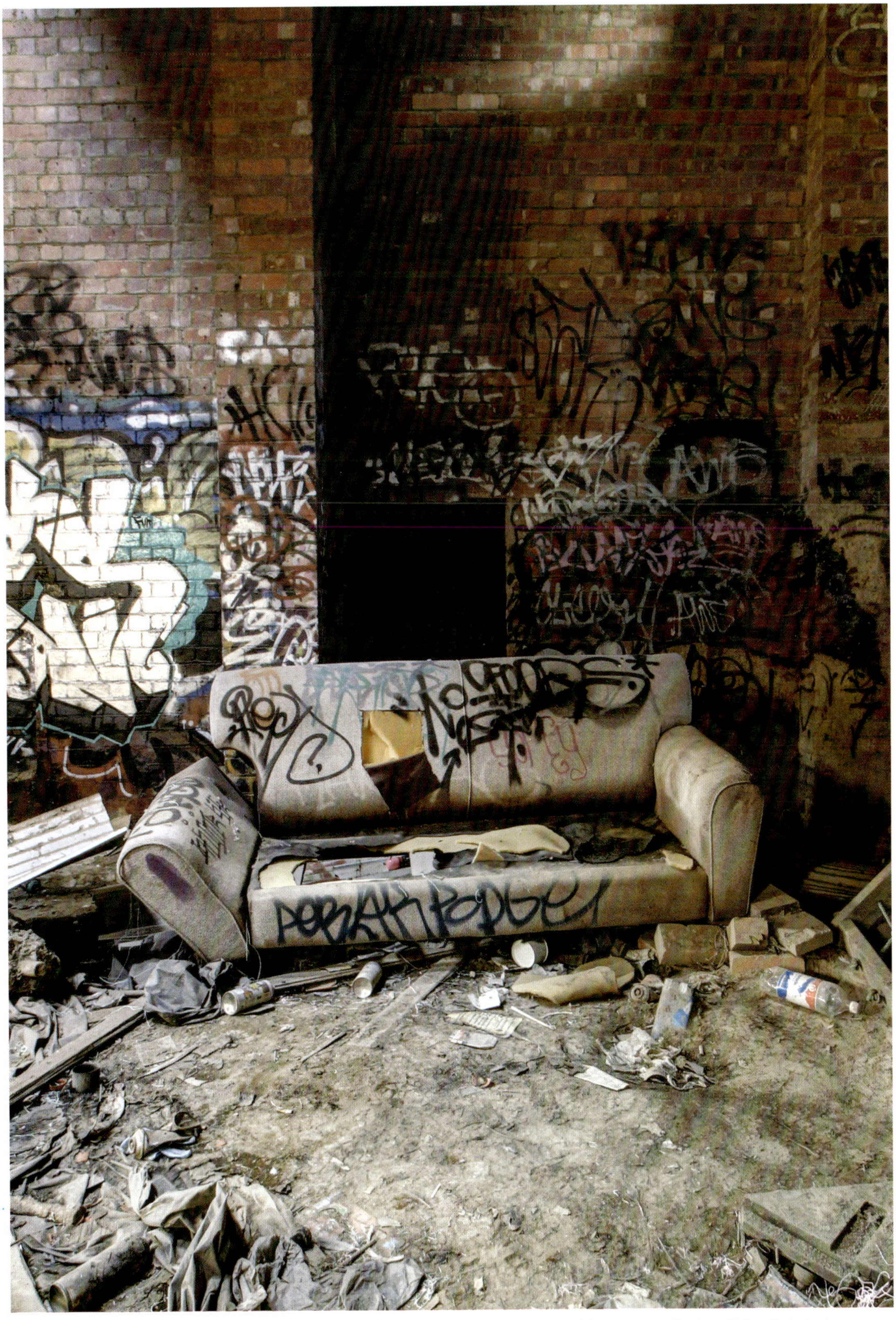

An old couch slumps in the shadows of the brick factory—worn and weathered, it once cradled graffiti artists taking breaks between bursts of colour and creativity.

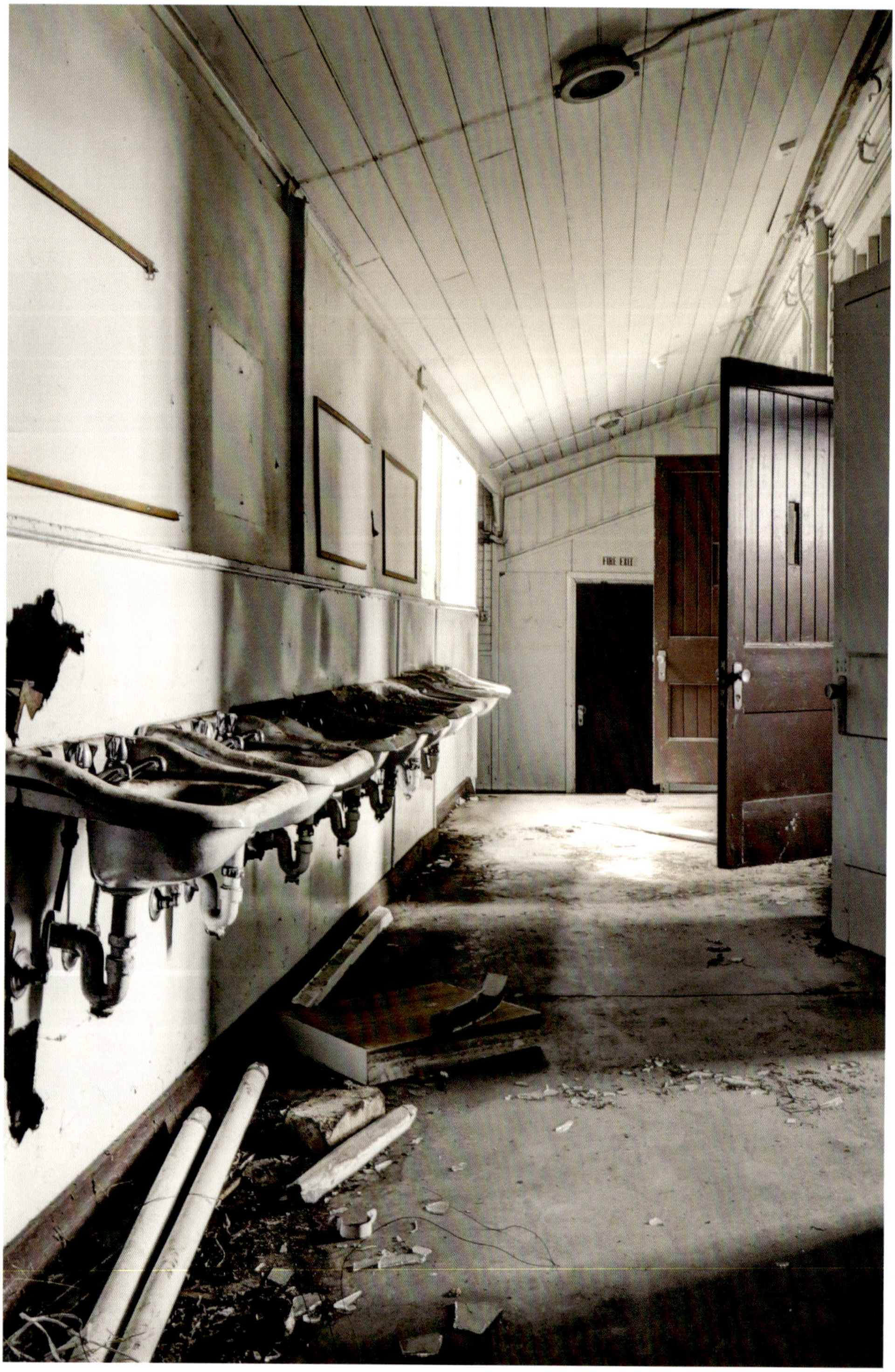

A row of wash basins sits adjacent to a line of observation cells, tracing a haunting passageway through the former Sunbury Asylum—echoes of routine etched into its decaying walls.

SUNBURY ASYLUM

The Sunbury Lunatic Asylum, established in the late 1800s, was one of Victoria's major 19th-century mental health institutions. Located in Sunbury, just outside Melbourne, the facility reflected the prevailing attitudes of the time, when mental illness was often equated with incurability and institutionalisation.

Throughout its long operational history, Sunbury Asylum's title and classification changed multiple times, mirroring broader social and legislative shifts in the understanding of mental illness. Between its opening and 1905, the institution was officially designated as an 'asylum', a term that reinforced the notion of containment over treatment. However, with the implementation of the Lunacy Act in the early 1900s, all asylums in Victoria were renamed 'hospitals for the insane', marking a symbolic move toward a more medicalised approach to mental health care (though in practice, the function and structure of Sunbury changed little).

Reclassification continued over the decades. Under the Mental Hygiene Act 1933, these institutions were renamed 'mental hospitals', and the evolving language reflected a growing awareness—though not necessarily a full transformation—of how mental health should be treated within society. Still, the core purpose of Sunbury remained largely the same: primarily housing long-term patients, often those considered beyond recovery. Temporary care was minimal, although 'receiving wards' were established for those requiring short-term care and evaluation.

Despite changes in terminology and the gradual progression in mental health treatment, Sunbury's operations remained deeply rooted in an outdated model of care. For most of its existence, it functioned less as a site of recovery and more as a place of exclusion for those deemed mentally unfit. Today, its buildings stand as a stark reminder of Victoria's psychiatric past, offering insight into both the evolution of mental health policy and the human cost of decades-long institutionalisation.

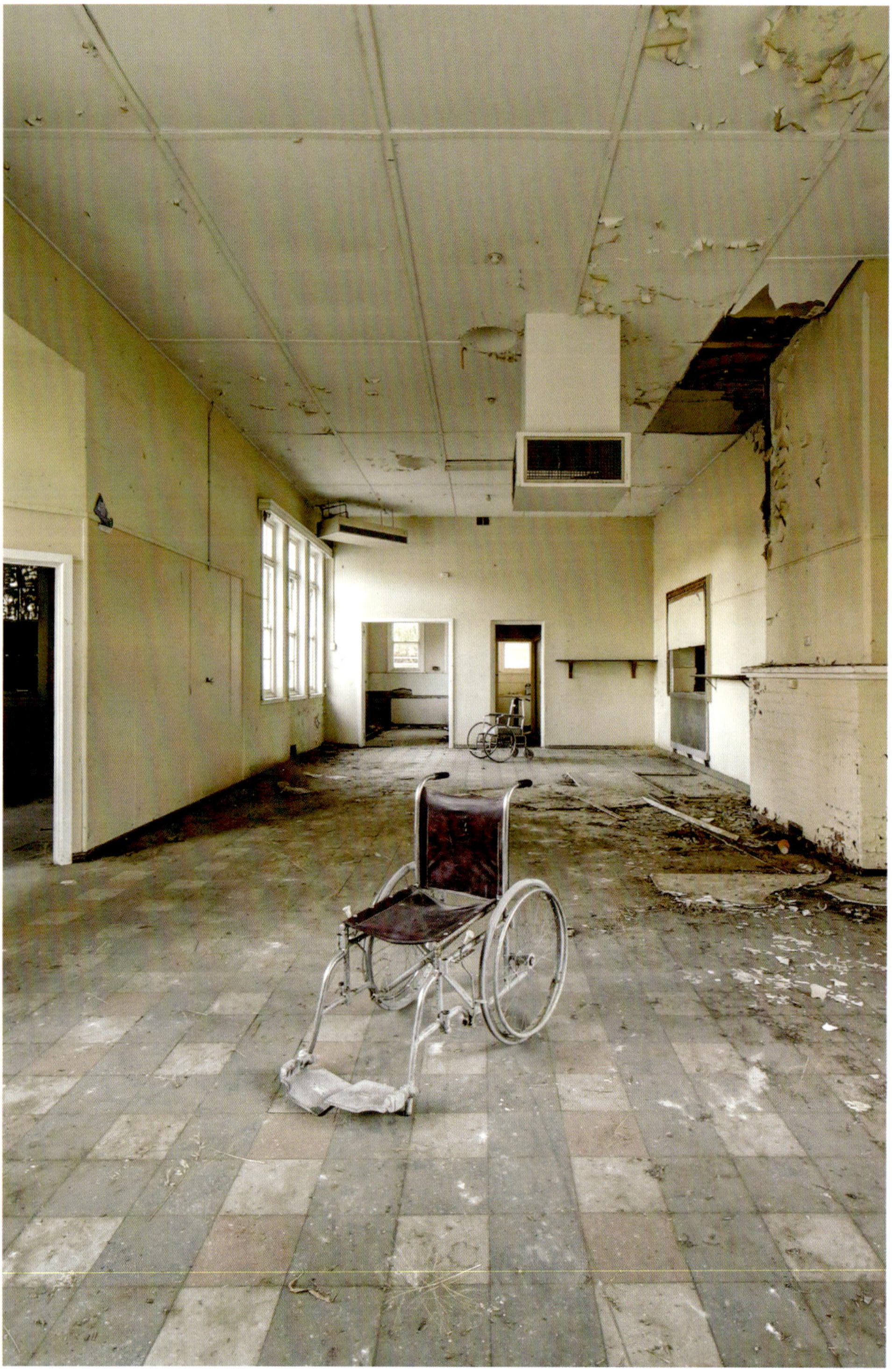

A lonely wheelchair sits silently in the entrance of the abandoned Pleasant Creek Hospital—a stark reminder of the patients and stories that once passed through its doors.

PLEASANT CREEK HOSPITAL

Stawell's Pleasant Creek Hospital was originally established in the late 19th century as a general hospital before transitioning into a specialised institution for people with intellectual and physical impairments. For much of the 20th century, it provided long-term residential care, reflecting the era's institutional model of support for those with complex needs.

The hospital ultimately closed in the 1990s amid broader reforms favouring community-based care. Since then, the abandoned site has become a well-known destination for urban explorers, with its haunting atmosphere attracting photographers and ghost hunters alike.

Still standing, the site serves as a quiet monument to the shifting ideals of healthcare and institutional practice in Victoria.

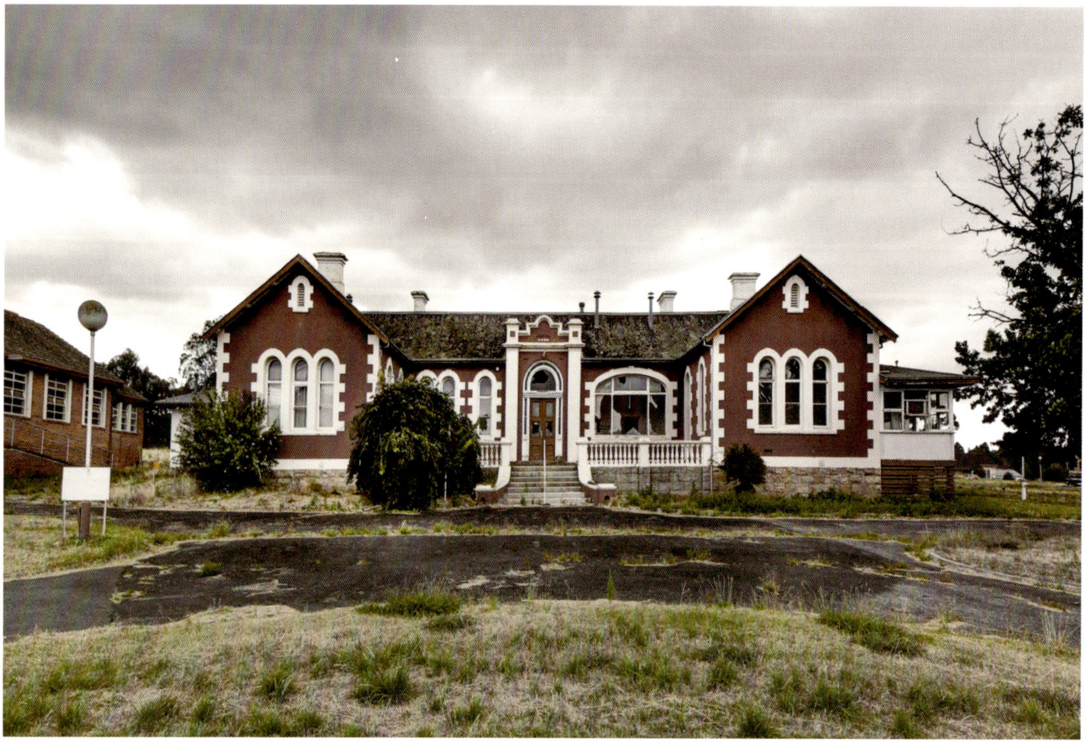

The front façade of Pleasant Creek Hospital looms haunting and ominous—its weathered exterior, reminiscent of a haunted asylum from a film set, draws in ghost hunters and the curious alike, eager to peer into its troubled past.

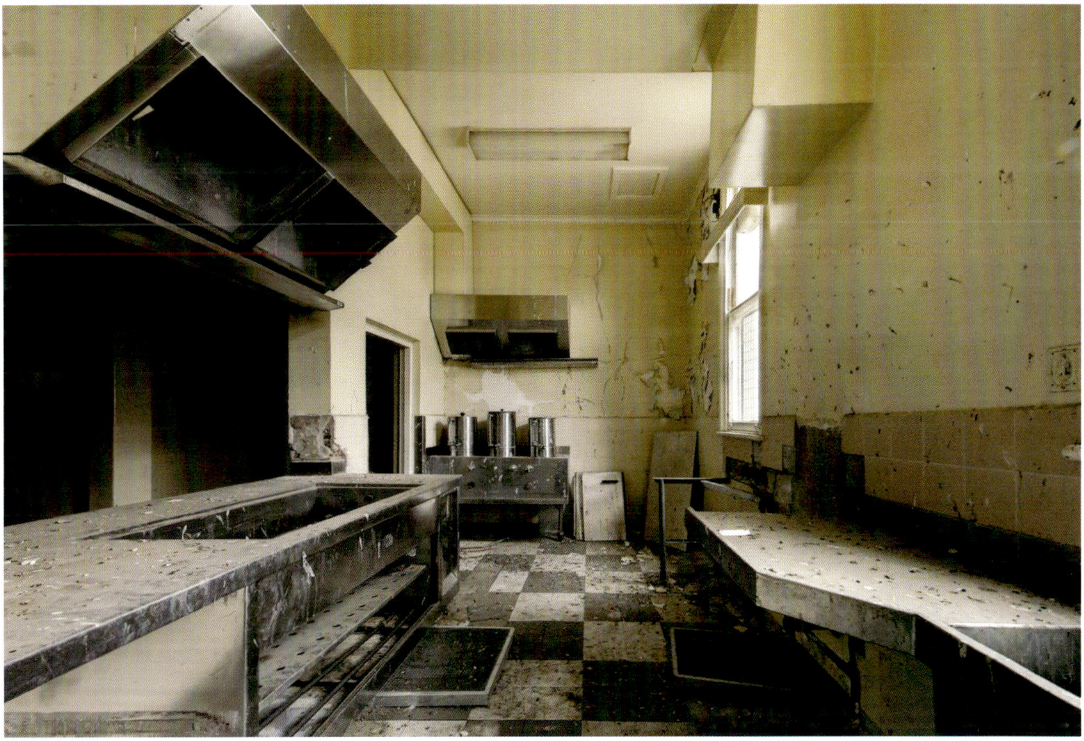

The hospital's former kitchen still holds relics of the past—rusted equipment and faded signs of routines long since abandoned.

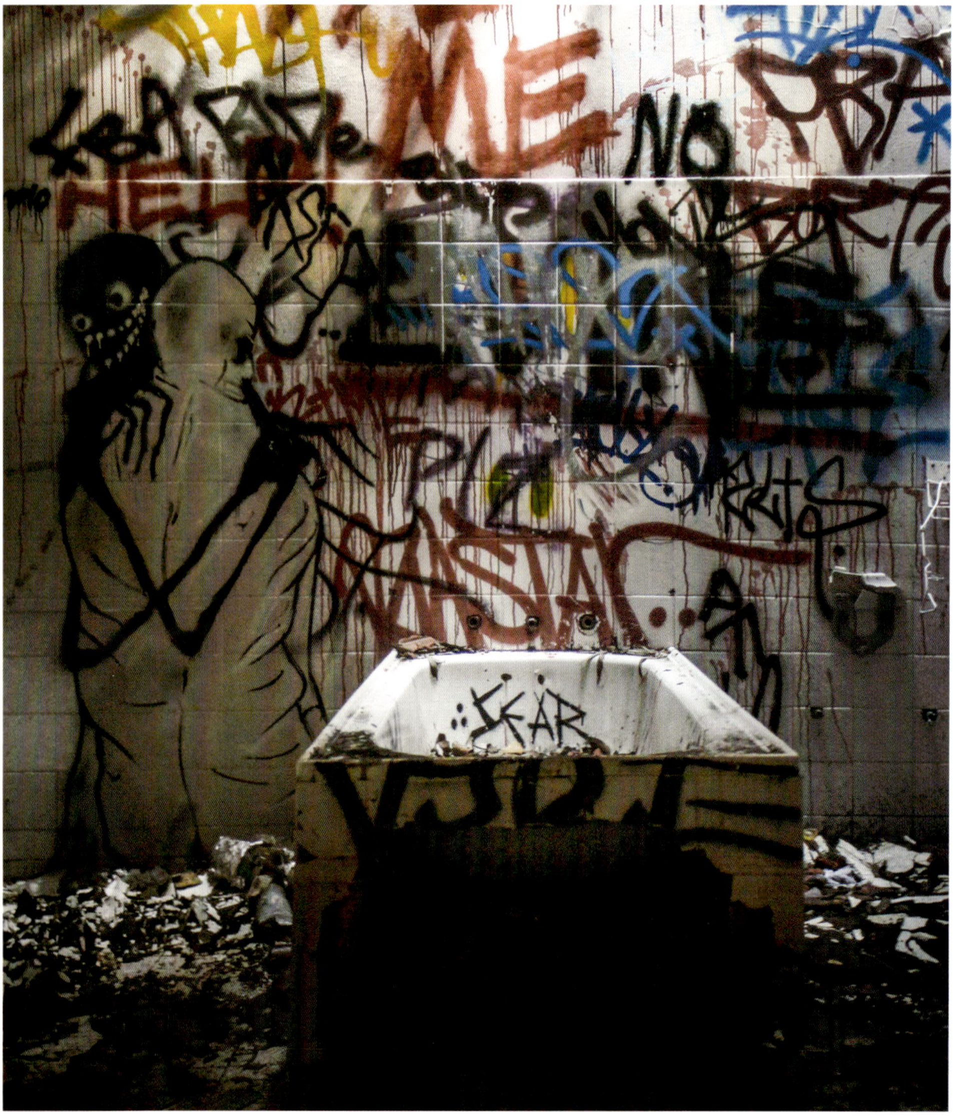

Just one of many macabre graffiti murals haunting the decaying rooms of Larundel Asylum—a chilling blend of art and abandonment.

LARUNDEL ASYLUM

Deep in Melbourne's northern suburbs, the minimal remains of Larundel Mental Hospital now stand as a skeletal echo of Victoria's shifting approach to psychiatric care. Built in the 1930s at the outset of World War II, Larundel was originally conceived as a replacement for the aging Kew Asylum. However, wartime necessity rerouted its initial purpose. During the war years, the partially completed buildings served multiple interim roles, most notably as a training facility for the Australian Air Force and, later, as temporary emergency housing.

In the 1950s, eight new rehabilitation wards were constructed, each capable of housing 45 patients. New nurses' homes were built along with two main admission wards to allow for mixed-sex treatment, a progressive step at the time. One of these admission wards was dedicated to younger patients, many diagnosed with schizophrenia who were undergoing insulin shock therapy, a common but controversial treatment of the period.

Part of the hospital was soon designated as a rehabilitation centre, aimed at individuals considered likely to reintegrate into society with further care. This addition reflected a gradual shift in the institutional mind-set—from indefinite containment toward the possibility of discharge and community-based recovery.

Decommissioned in the 1990s, the asylum became a legendary site for urban explorers, photographers and ghost hunter enthusiasts alike. Its decaying halls, peeling walls and graffiti-smeared rooms offered a hauntingly atmospheric backdrop that stirred the imagination and invited creative expression. The asylum's dark and gloomy presence—shaped by decades of abandonment and whispered histories—made it a compelling destination for those drawn to forgotten spaces and the stories they hold. For many, Larundel was more than just a derelict building; it was a stage where curiosity, creativity and a touch of the macabre could freely thrive.

Adding to the eerie atmosphere was the asylum's dense layering of dark-themed graffiti, which transformed Larundel into something akin to an unintentional theme park-like haunted house or ghost train. Stark images of skulls, cryptic messages and surreal, nightmarish figures loomed from the walls, guiding visitors through a maze of visual unease. Each corridor seemed to tell its own twisted story, blending the real-life decay of the building with imagined horrors sprayed in bold colour. This fusion of art and ruin intensified the sense of disorientation and thrill, making every turn feel like a step deeper into a haunted labyrinth.

Remembered by many as a Melbournian youth '*Halloween-thrill ride*' rite-of-passage, navigating Larundel wasn't just about exploration—it was an immersive and playfully macabre sensory experience where reality blurred with urban legend.

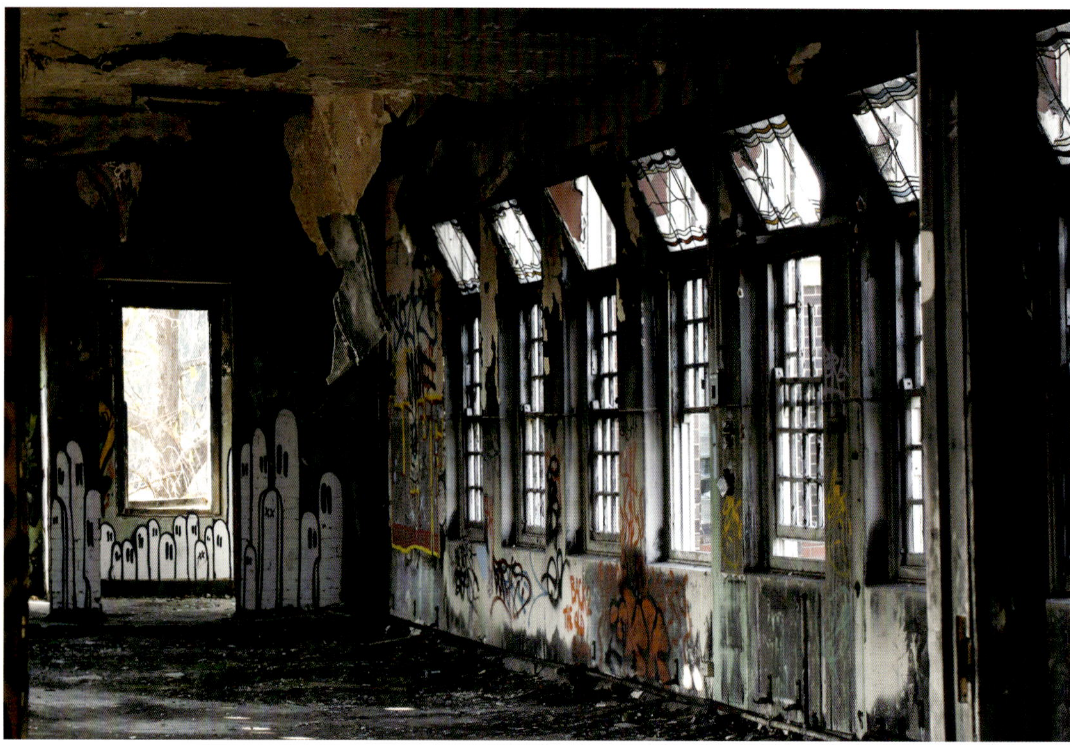

Creative graffiti transformed Larundel into an unofficial underground street art gallery—where decay and expression collided in vivid, unsettling harmony.

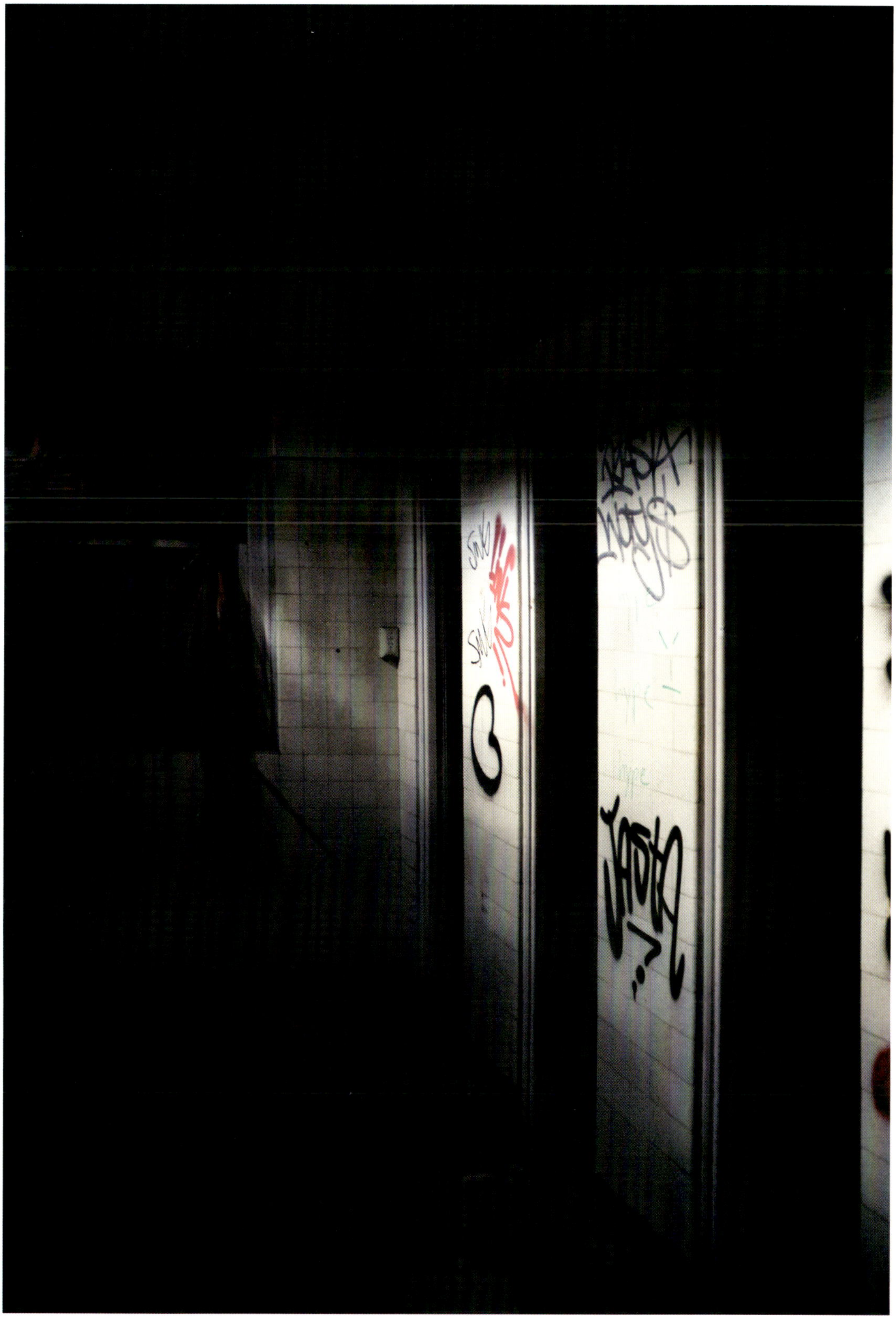

One of Larundel Asylum's eerie washrooms—its cracked tiles and rusted fixtures seem to echo with the lingering whispers of those long departed.

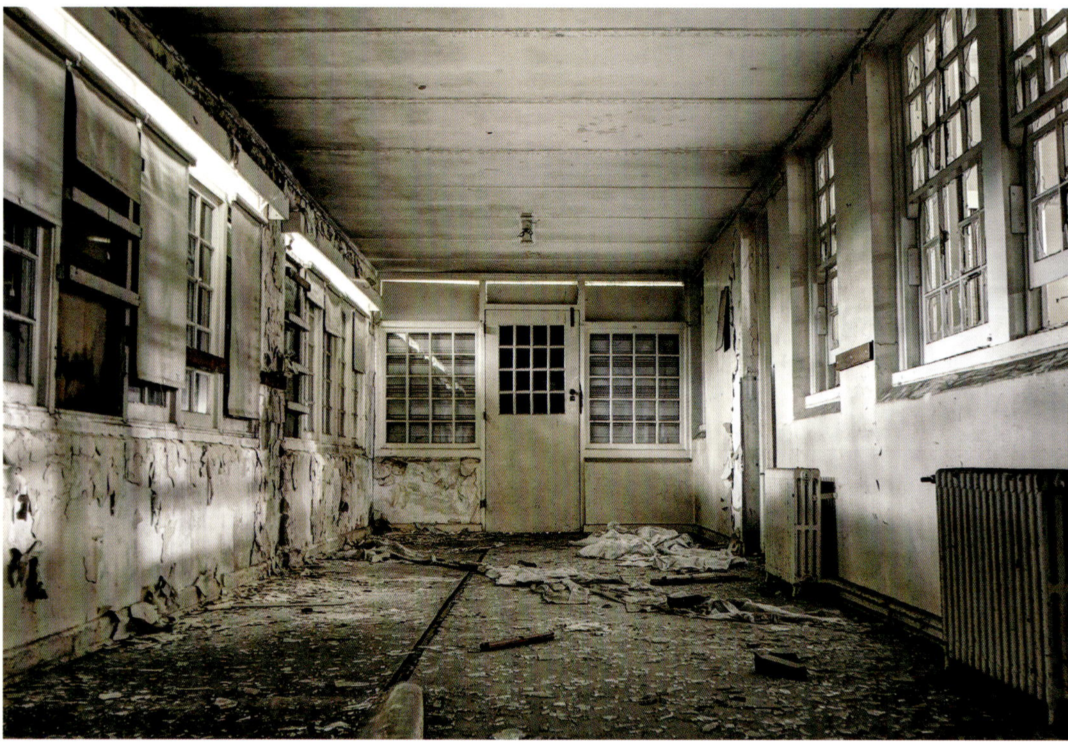

Boarded up for years, this shadowy space at the rear of the complex is cloaked in peeling paint—each flake a quiet testament to time, neglect, and forgotten purpose.

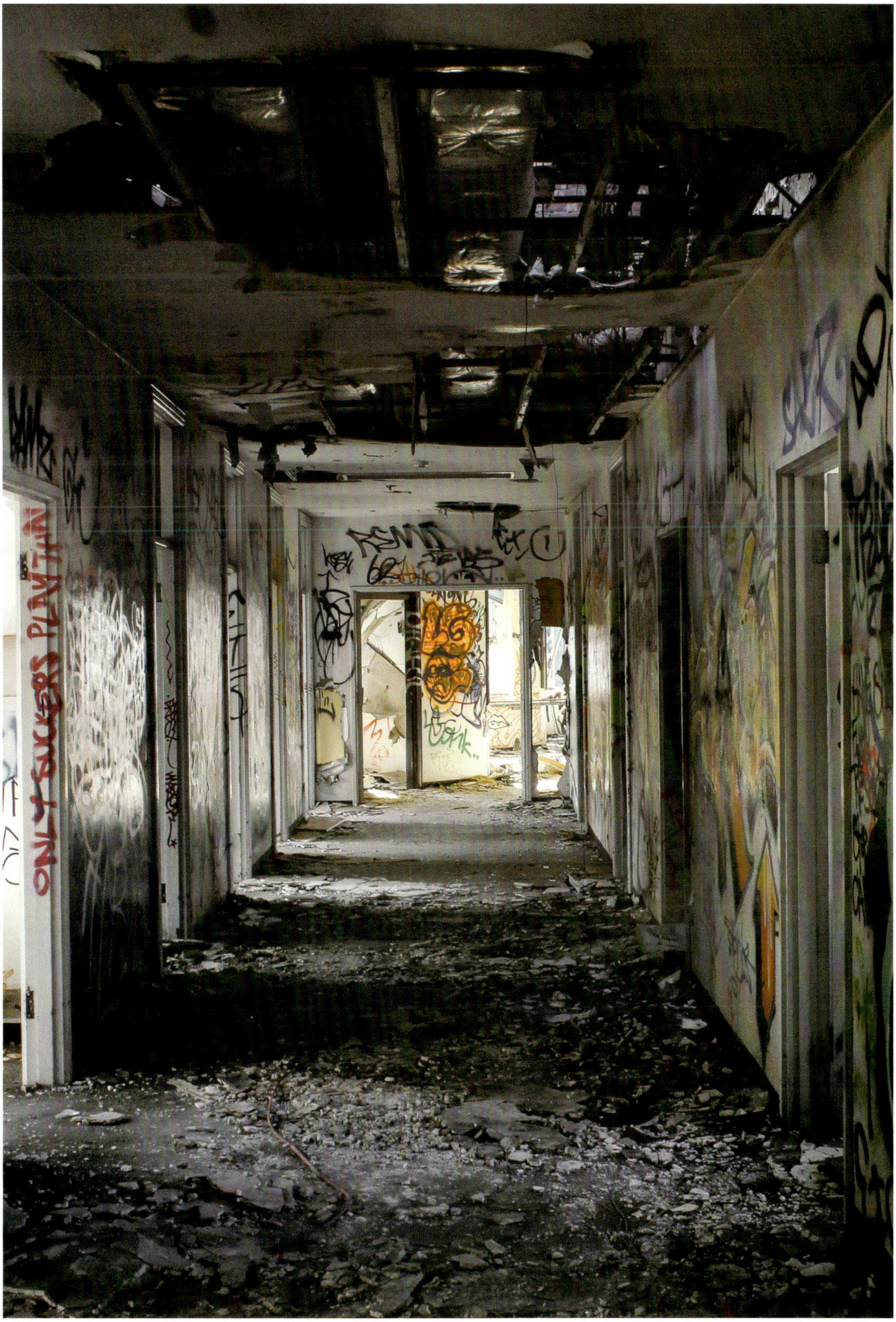

One of Larundel Asylum's many graffiti-covered hallways. These decaying corridors became an infamous feature of the derelict complex, where art and abandonment coexisted perfectly.

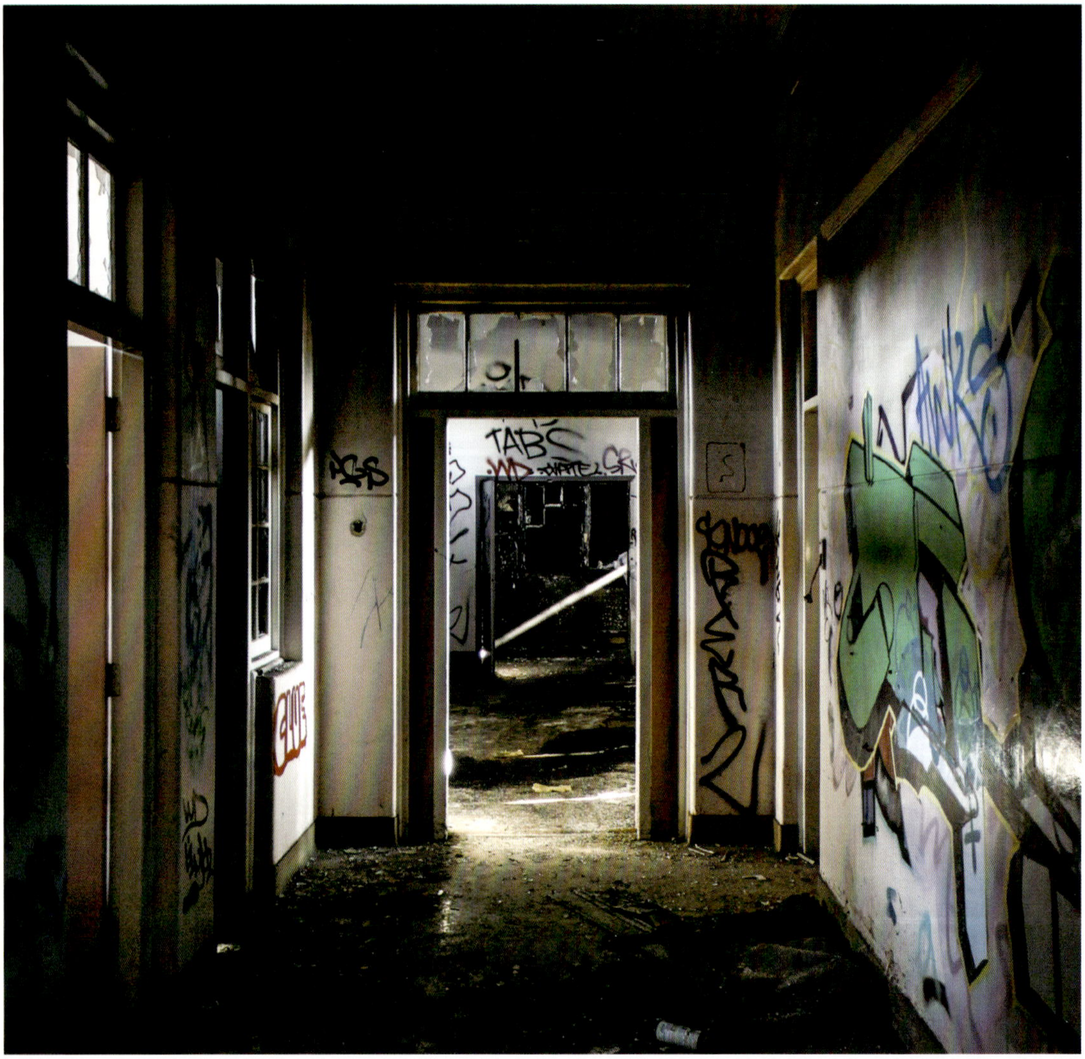

A labyrinthine network of intricate passageways linked each section of the asylum. Now cloaked in graffiti and decay, it was easy for an explorer to lose their way in this haunted maze.

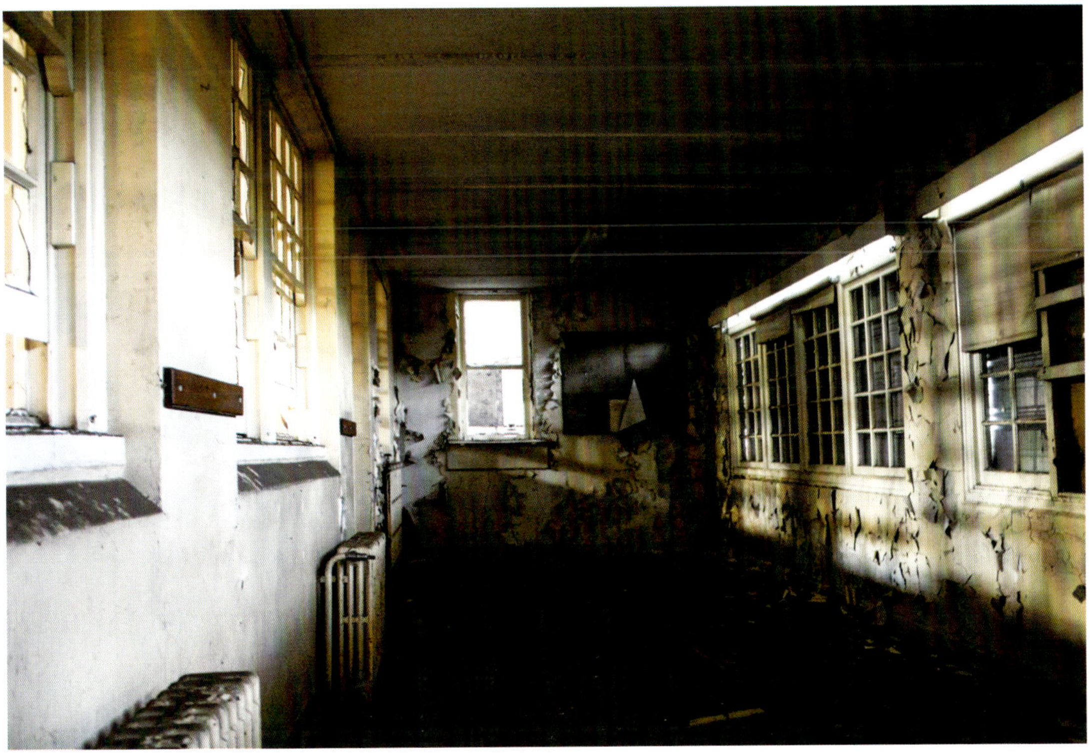

Vintage heaters, scattered throughout the asylum's dark hallways, were among the last enduring relics—silent reminders of the lives once kept warm within these cold, institutional walls.

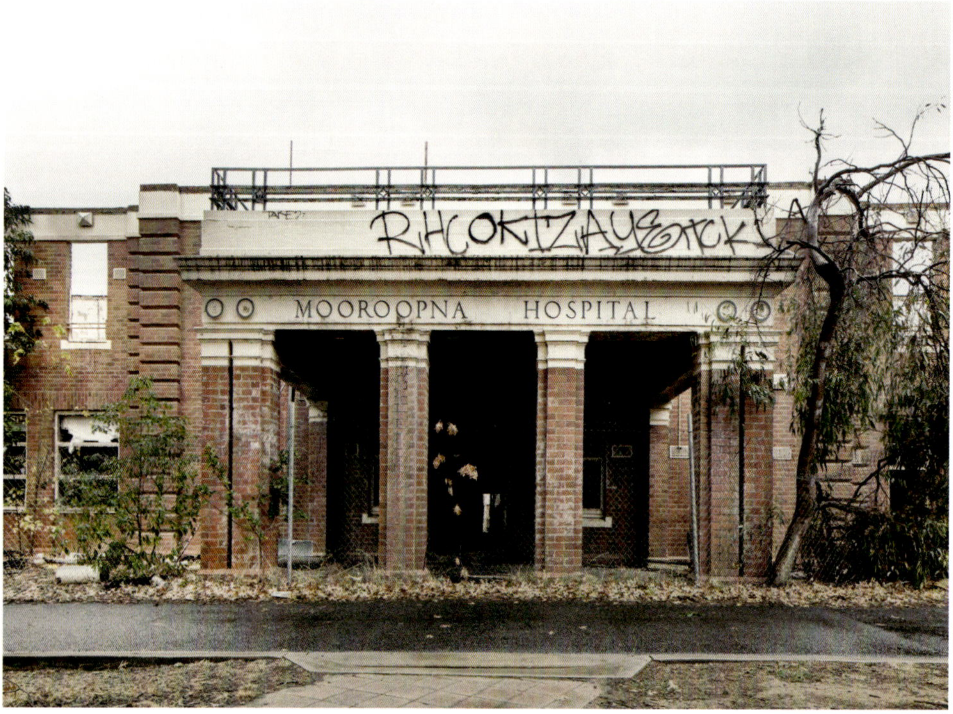

The front façade of the long-abandoned Mooroopna Hospital stands as a scorched remnant of the past—moderately intact despite the fire that gutted the rest of the facility, it hints at the structure that once was.

MOOROOPNA HOSPITAL

Mooroopna Hospital was a key healthcare facility serving the Greater Shepparton community. Originally established in the mid-20th century, the hospital played a crucial role in providing medical care, particularly for workers in the nearby agricultural and fruit-growing industries.

Operations were transferred to the modern Goulburn Valley Health facility in Shepparton, leading to the hospital's permanent closure. Since then, the abandoned site has fallen into disrepair, becoming a target for vandalism, arson and urban exploration. Its decaying buildings and eerie atmosphere have made it a well-known local landmark.

Despite various discussions about redevelopment, the site remains in a derelict state, standing as a reminder of Mooroopna's medical history and the challenges of repurposing abandoned infrastructure in regional areas.

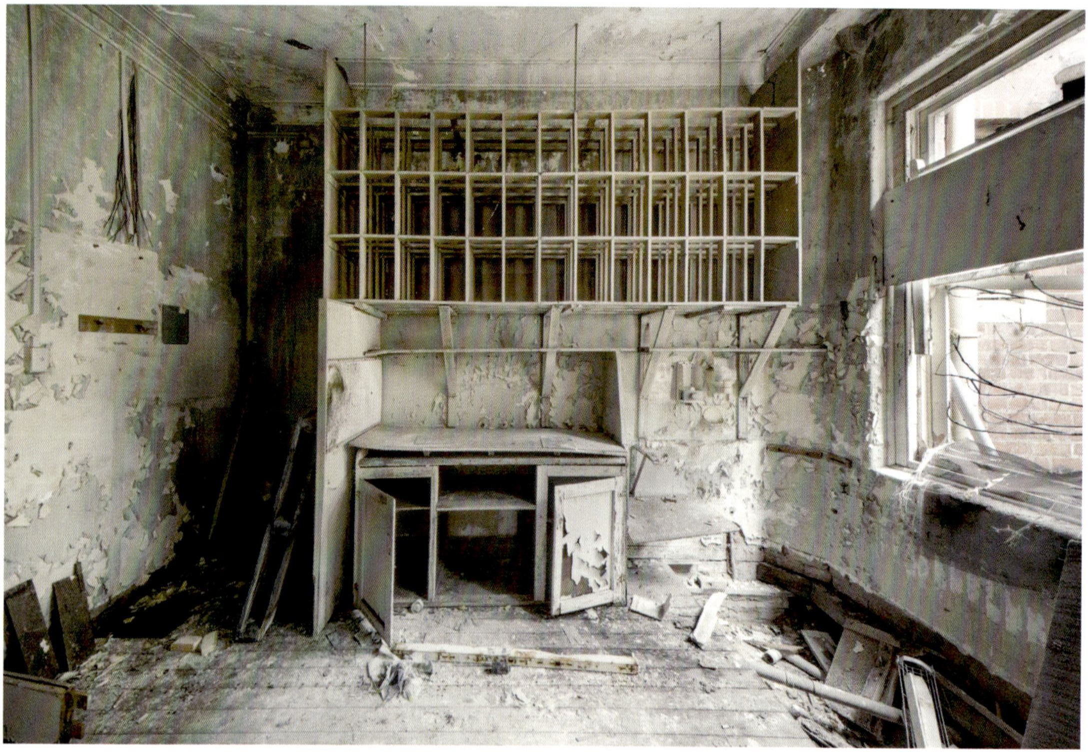

This room once held patient records—its walls, now crumbling, once safeguarded the intimate details of countless lives who passed through the hospital's care.

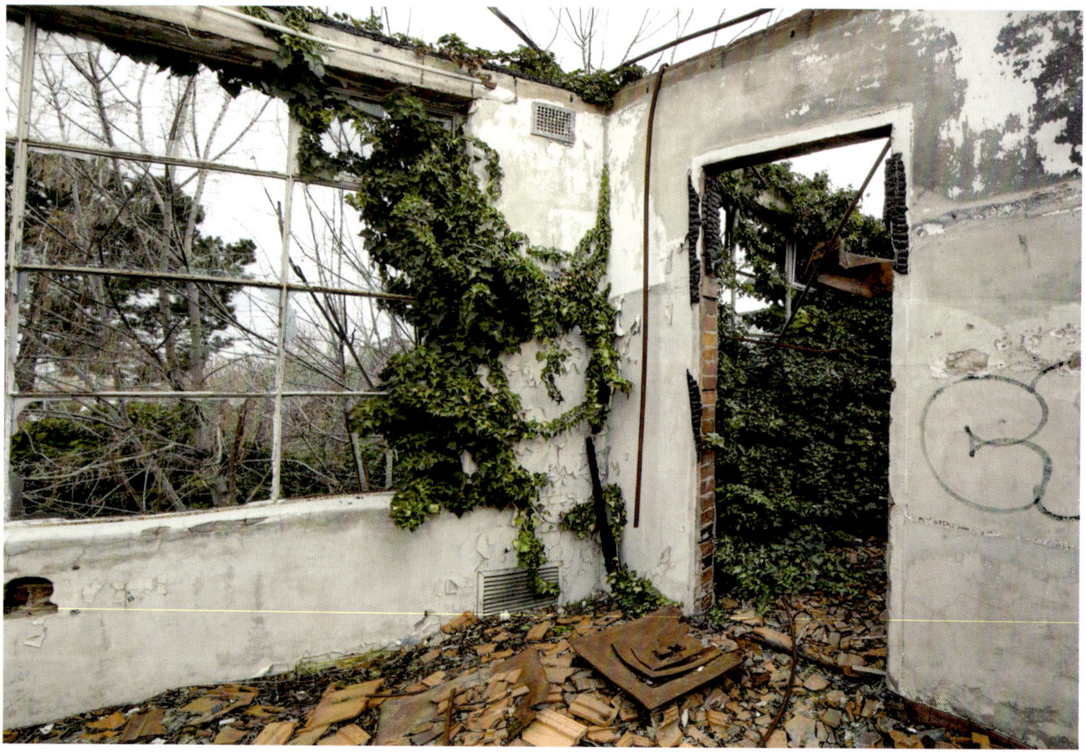

Mooroopna Hospital's upper level succumbed to fire in 2011, leaving behind skeletal remains of its former structure.

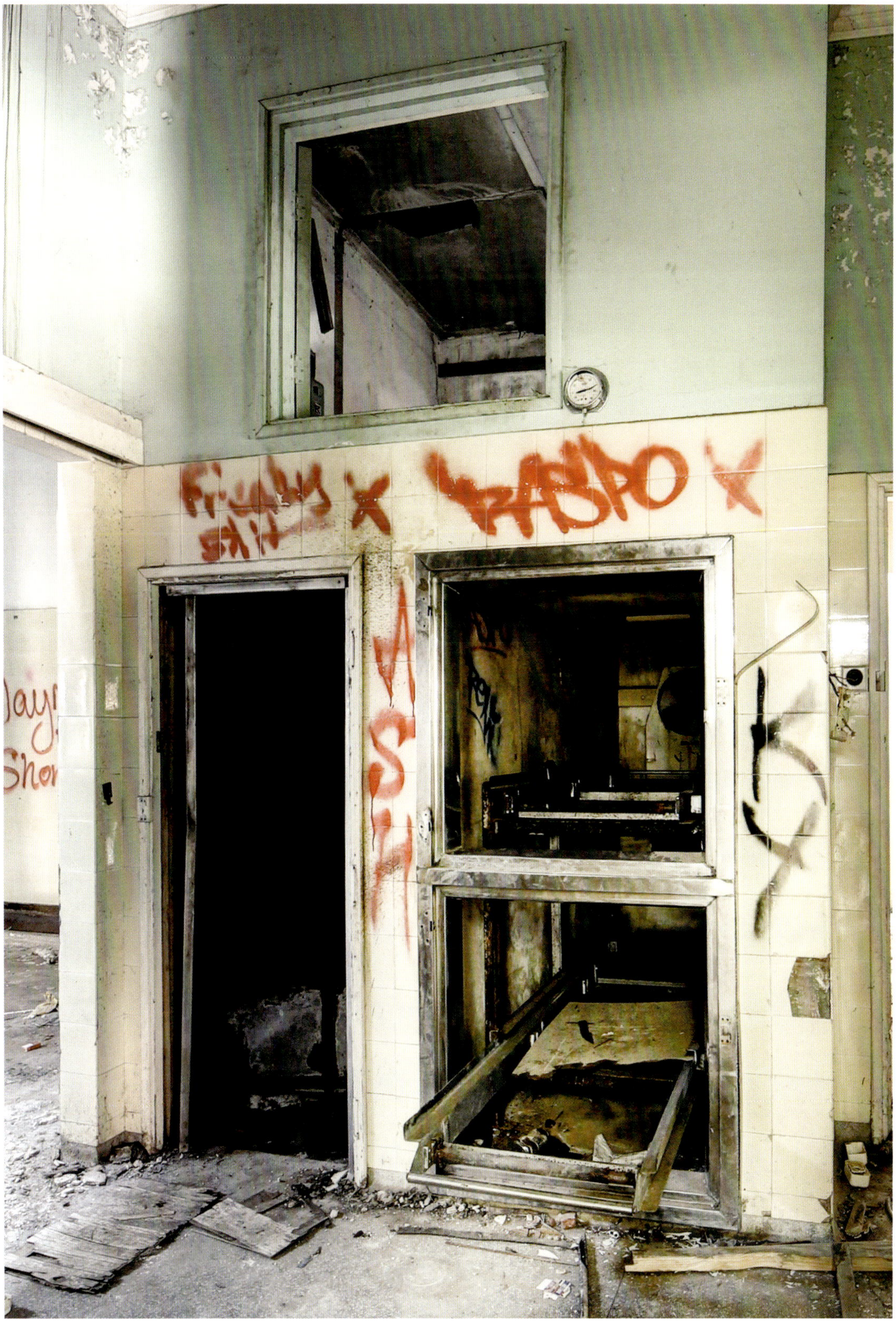

One of the hospital's most morbid areas—the morgue—still holds the skeletal remains of its original mortuary cabinet and drawers, silent witnesses to the facility's darkest duties.

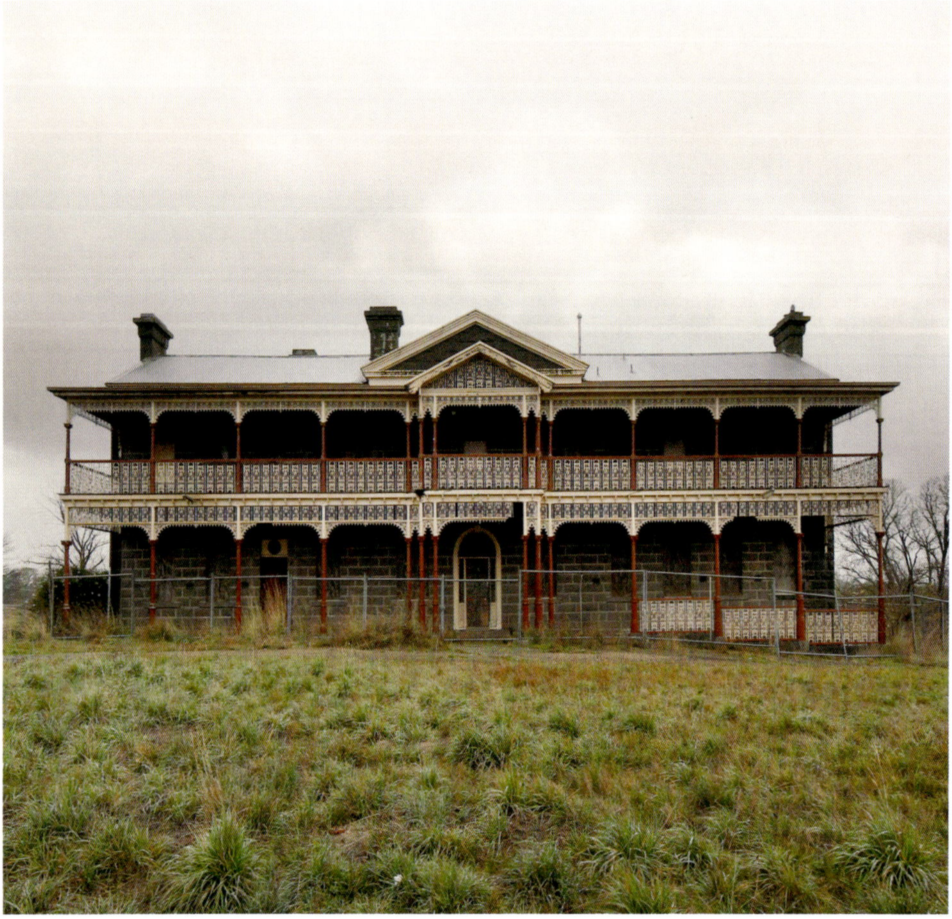

Kyneton's old hospital casts a brooding shadow over the quiet town.

KYNETON HOSPITAL

Kyneton Hospital, in the Macedon Ranges, was originally built in the 19th century and served as a vital medical facility for the local community for over a century. With its historic architecture and long-standing role in regional healthcare, the hospital was an important institution for Kyneton and surrounding areas.

In the late 20th century, medical services were relocated to a more modern facility, leading to the hospital's closure. Since then, the site has remained abandoned, with its deteriorating buildings attracting urban explorers, historians and ghost hunters due to its eerie atmosphere and reports of paranormal activity.

While there have been discussions about redevelopment, the hospital's future remains uncertain. The site stands as a relic of Kyneton's medical history, reflecting broader changes in rural healthcare infrastructure over time.

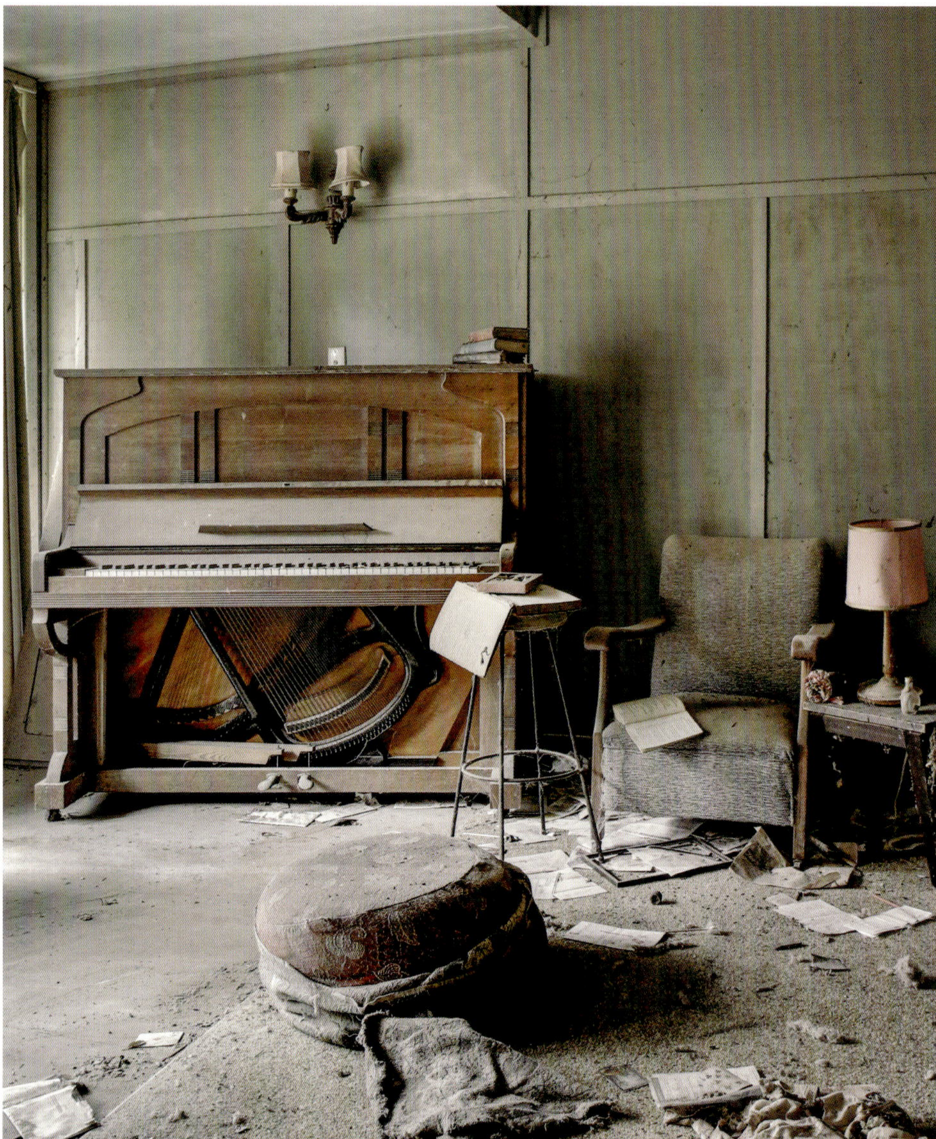

This abandoned house featured a piano and vintage furniture, with wartime-coloured walls that added a nostalgic, timeworn charm to the space.

ABANDONED HOUSING

Across the Victorian landscape, abandoned homes—both rural and urban, stand as mute observers of the state's evolving and demanding relationship with land and housing. In the countryside, weather-beaten homesteads lie scattered through farmland and bush, their cracked walls and rusted roofs telling stories of families who built entire lives from soil and sweat. Many date back to the 19th and early 20th centuries, constructed by settlers, pastoralists and gold rush-era opportunists who etched their existence into Victoria's agricultural and colonial frontier. These homes were tied to sheep stations, wheat fields and dairy farms.

But as decades passed, droughts lingered, industries mechanised and rural populations drained toward the cities. Homesteads were left behind—gradually reclaimed by nature. Some became ruinous curiosities; others remained eerily suspended in a moment long gone. Their emptiness speaks of both environmental hardship, as regional sustainability gave way to consolidation and urban sprawl.

Yet, abandonment is not just a rural phenomenon. In Melbourne's inner suburbs—areas that are gripped by soaring property values and rental scarcity—a number of vacant houses sit quietly behind boarded-up windows. Many of these homes are caught in legal disputes, land banking, speculative investment or slow redevelopment timelines. Some have been unoccupied for years. In neighbourhoods where rental queues stretch around the block and public housing lists grow longer by the day, the sight of these inner-city voids is a stark contradiction.

The irony is impossible to ignore. Victoria is in the midst of an escalating housing crisis, with thousands unable to secure stable or affordable accommodation, yet it is also home to a number of abandoned dwellings—homes that once sheltered families, dreams and community. From bluestone cottages in Melbourne's backstreets to timber farmhouses crumbling into paddocks, these places serve as visual reminders of a system that has perhaps prioritised profit over access.

For photographers, urban explorers and historians, these sites offer a compelling window into the past. But for the broader public, they should raise questions about the present: how did we arrive at a point where homes are left to rot while people sleep rough in our cities? What futures could these places hold—if not just as artefacts, but as part of a more compassionate housing strategy?

The forgotten homes of Victoria are more than ruins. They are quiet indictments of policy failure, cautionary tales of impermanence and, perhaps, opportunities for reimagining how we value space and the fundamental right to a home.

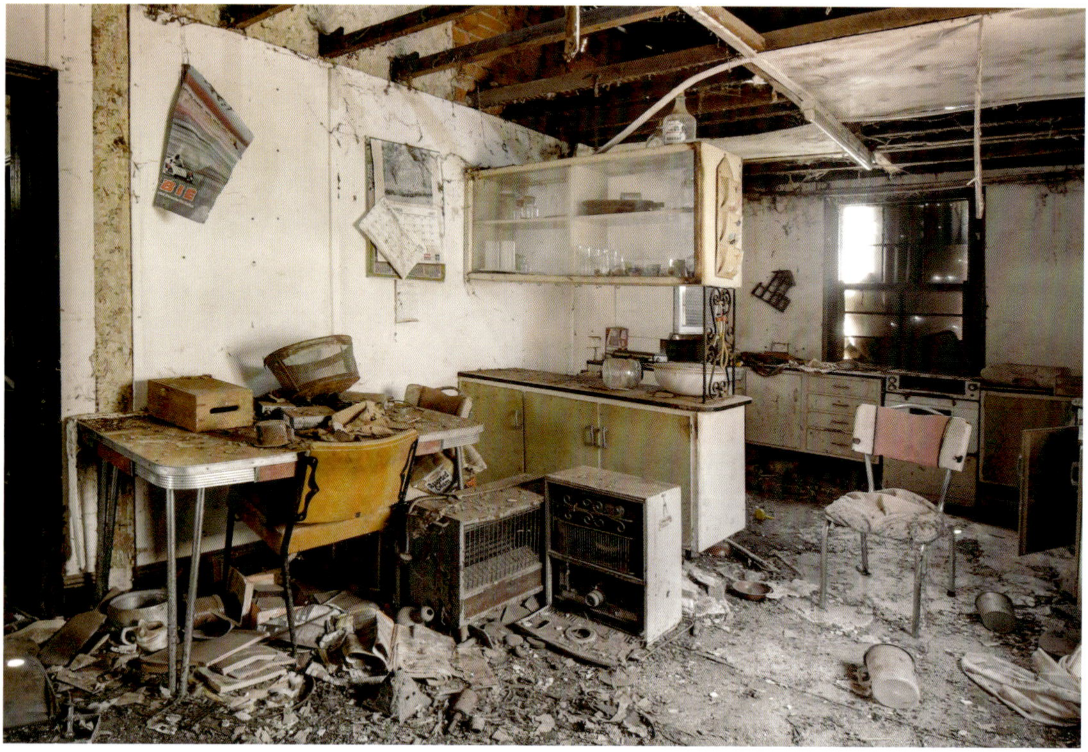

This interior included a vintage suspended glass and plate cabinet—a common feature in many mid 20th century kitchens.

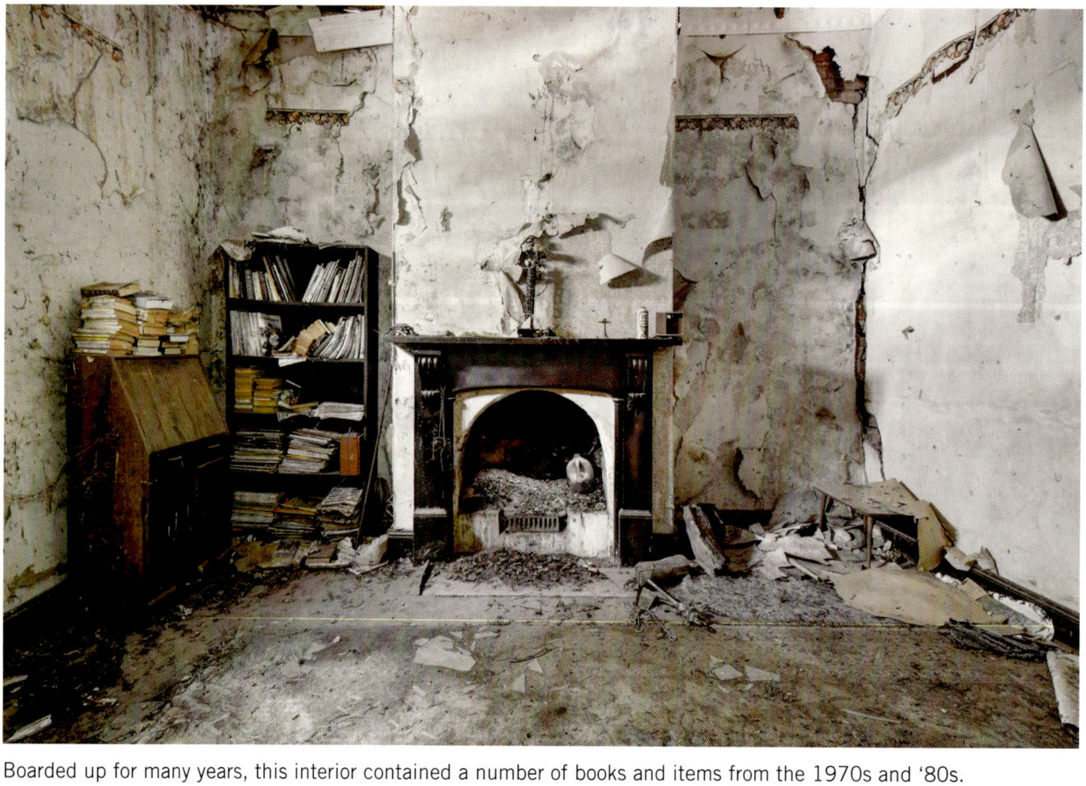

Boarded up for many years, this interior contained a number of books and items from the 1970s and '80s.

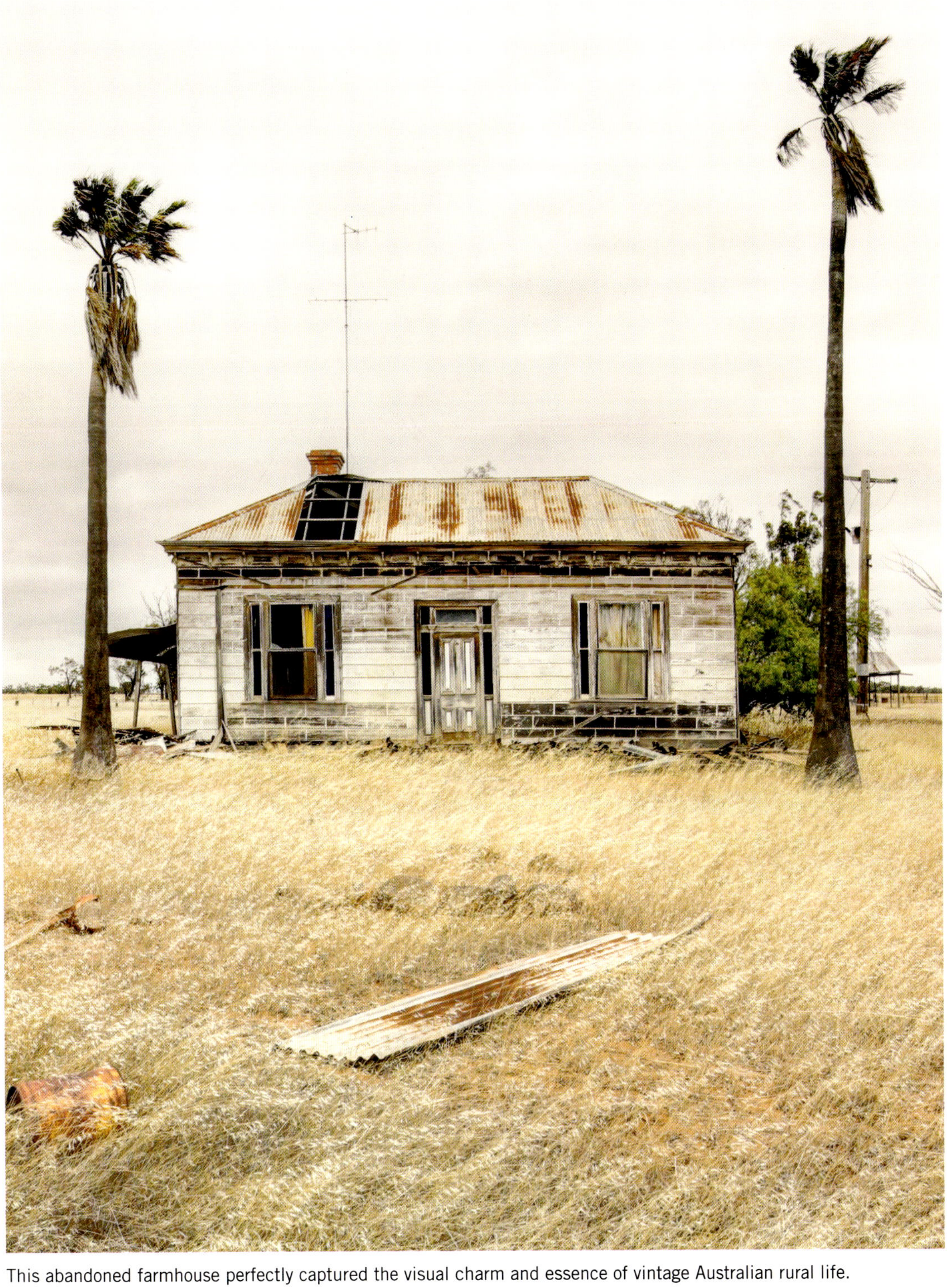

This abandoned farmhouse perfectly captured the visual charm and essence of vintage Australian rural life.

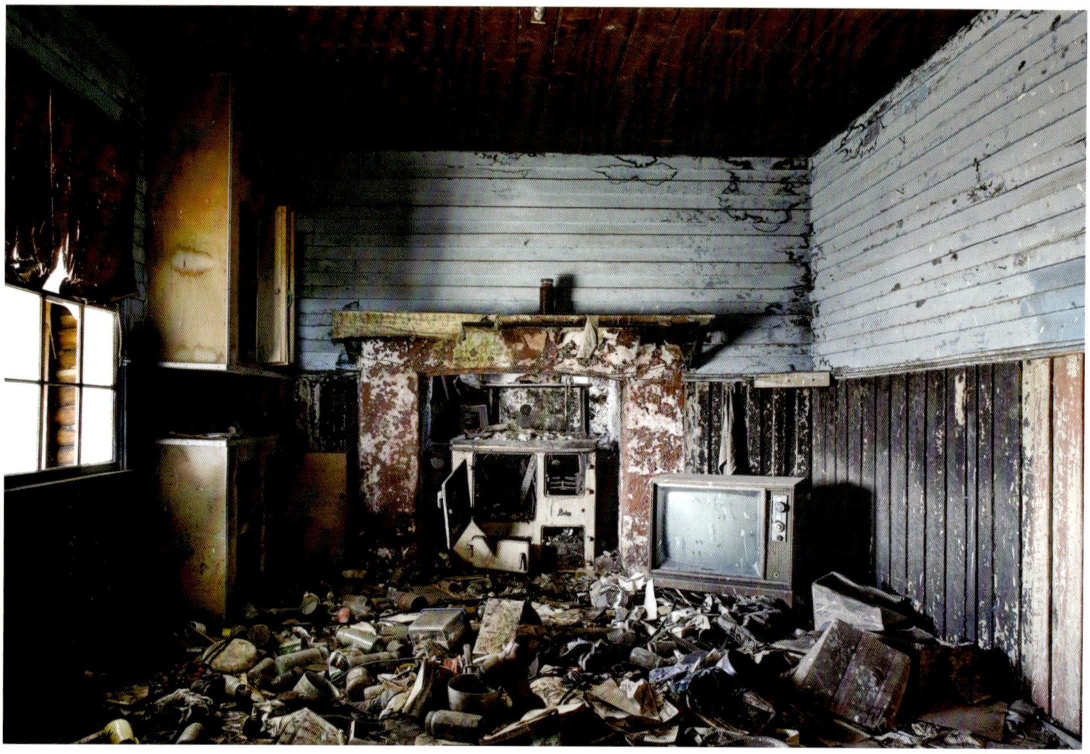

This farmhouse was strewn with household relics, its dusty interior anchored by a vintage TV set tucked quietly into one corner—a forgotten window to another era.

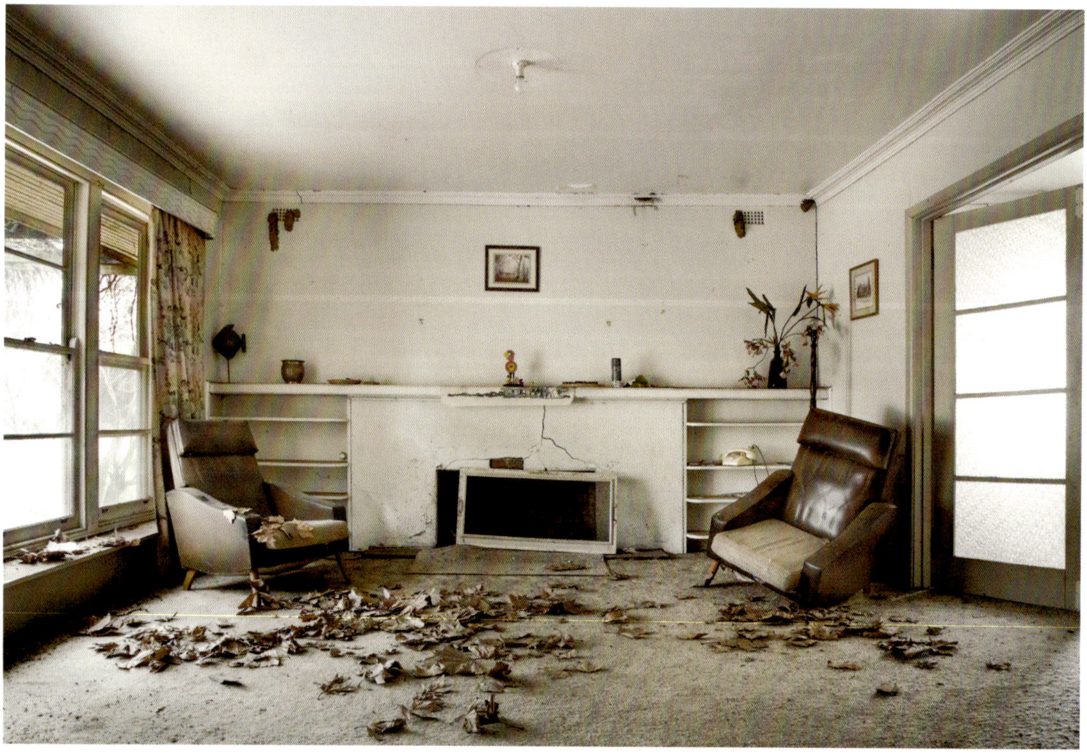

The lounge of this discarded house featured vintage armchairs slowly succumbing to decay, while wasps' nests emerged from its air vents—nature reclaiming comfort once carefully arranged.

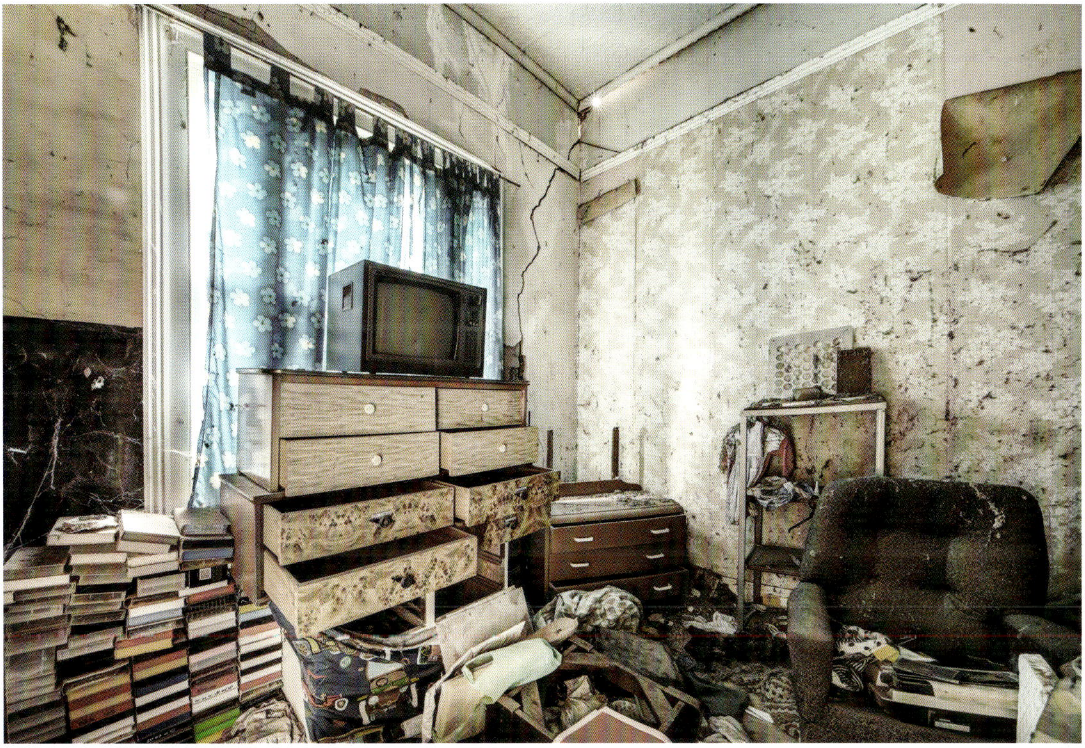

This bedroom still contained a stack of VHS cassettes, now draped in cobwebs—fragile remnants of a time when stories were rewound, not streamed.

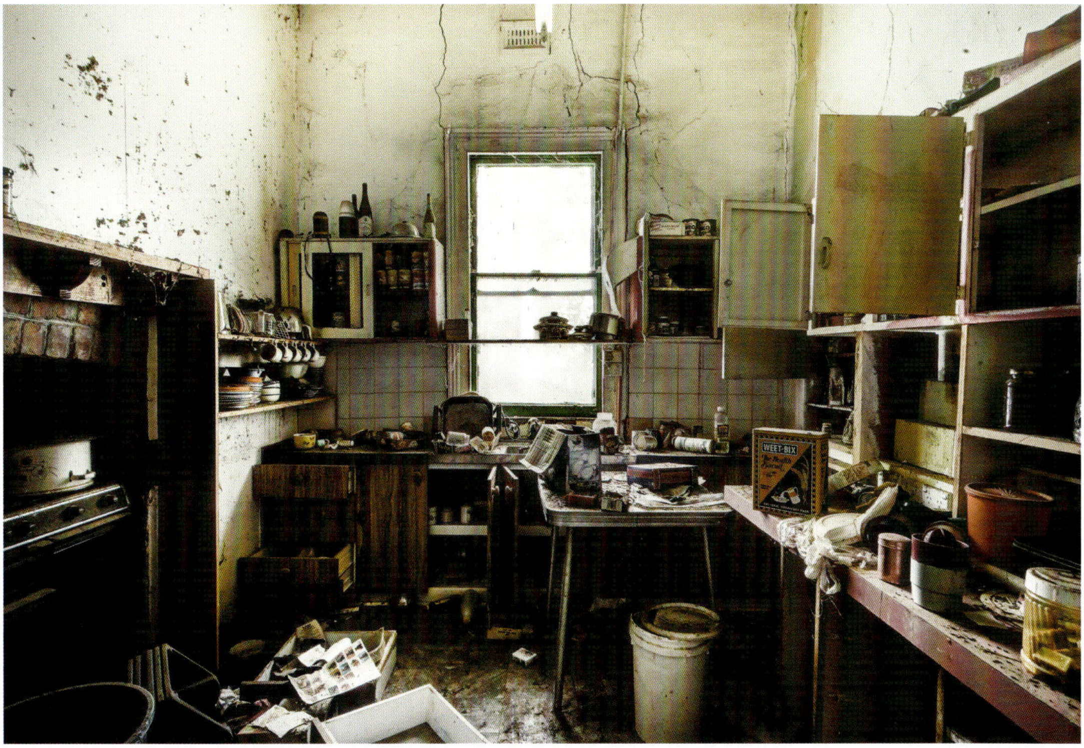

This kitchen remained eerily intact—drawers filled with cutlery and cooking items, while the pantry still held packages of long-expired food, frozen in time like a meal never made.

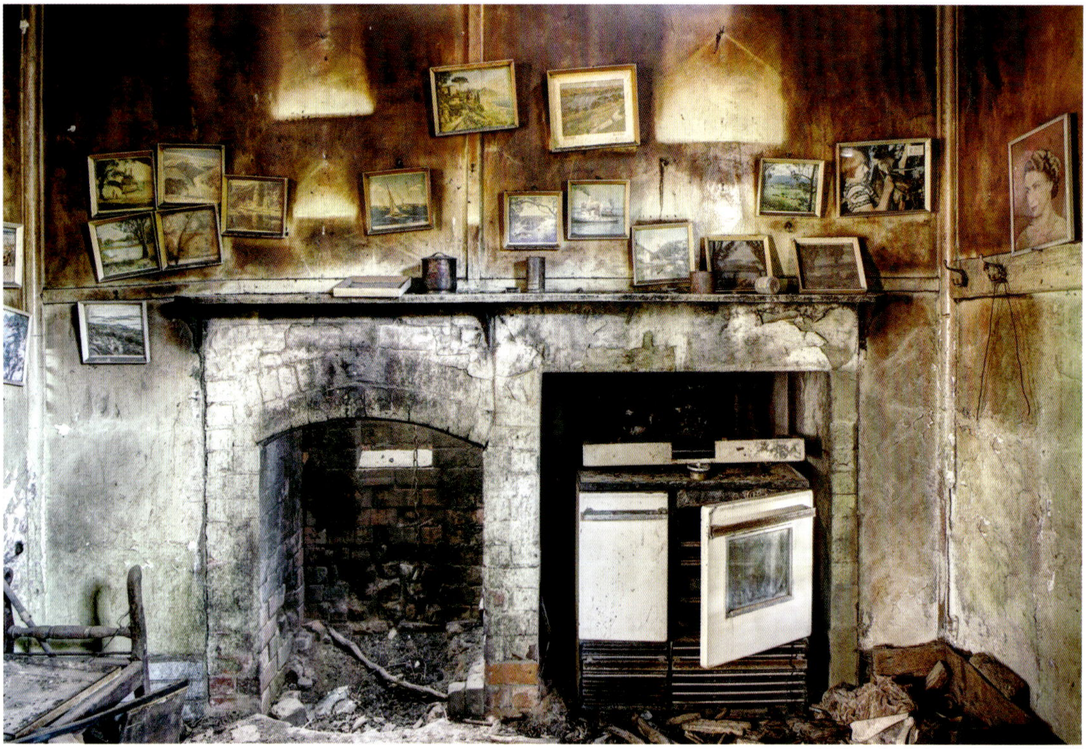

This old rustic kitchen retained all its original fittings, with a collection of faded paintings and pictures still hanging on the walls—quietly enduring and untouched after many years.

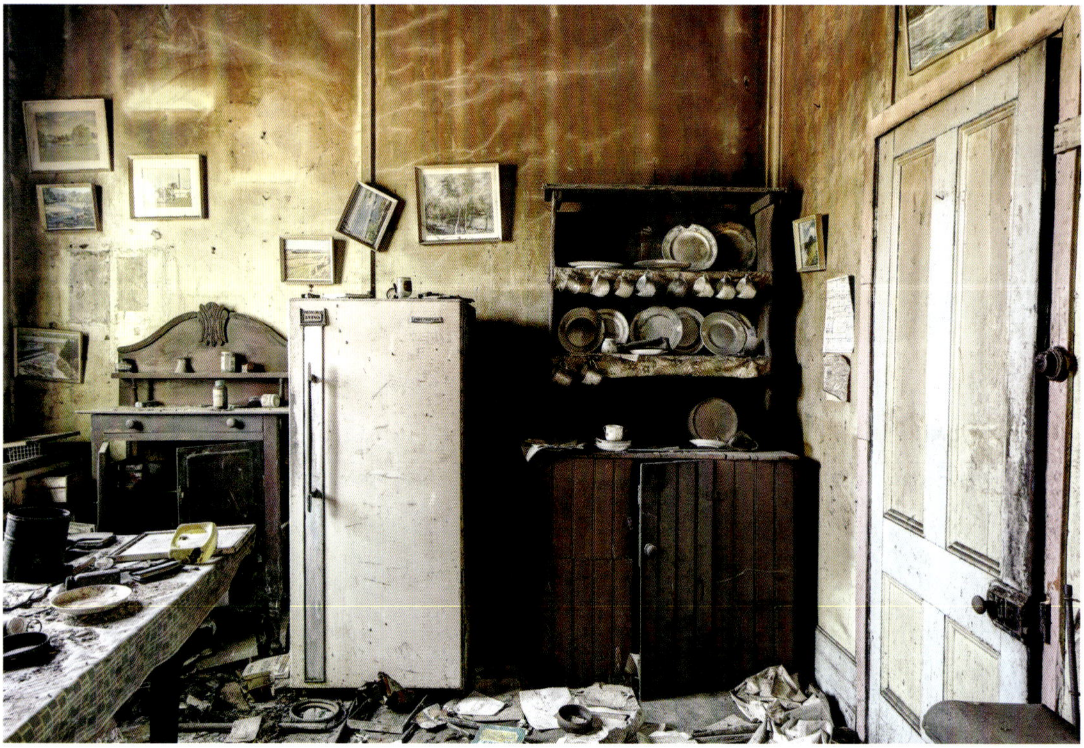

The kitchen's original fridge sat like an orphan left behind—its once vital presence now cold, silent, and forgotten amid the dust.

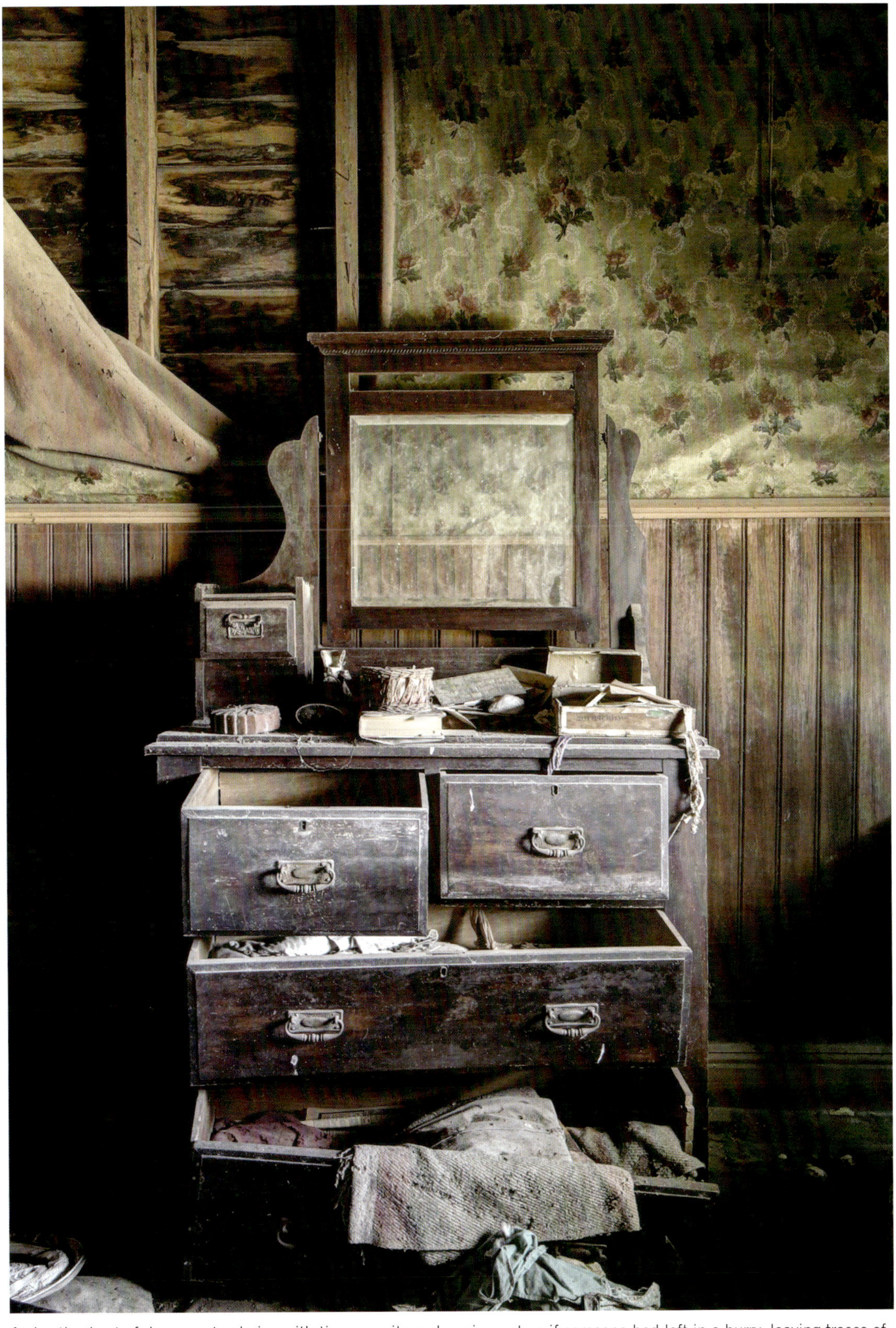

A ghostly chest of drawers stood ajar, with timeworn items hanging out as if someone had left in a hurry, leaving traces of a life paused, but never resumed.

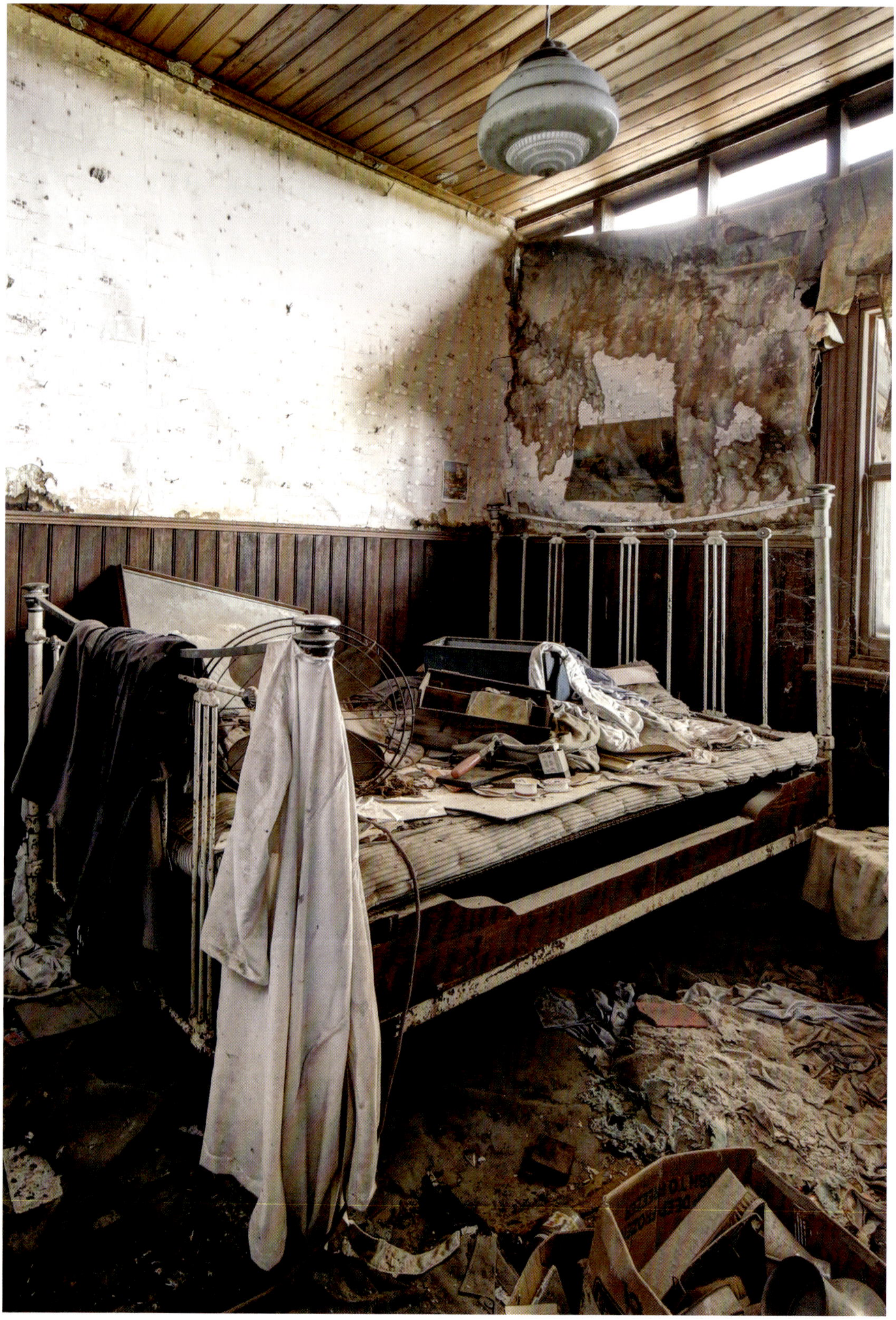

A waterlogged bed sat heavy with damp and decay, still covered in bedroom items left behind by its former occupant—intimate remnants of a life slowly dissolving into ruin.

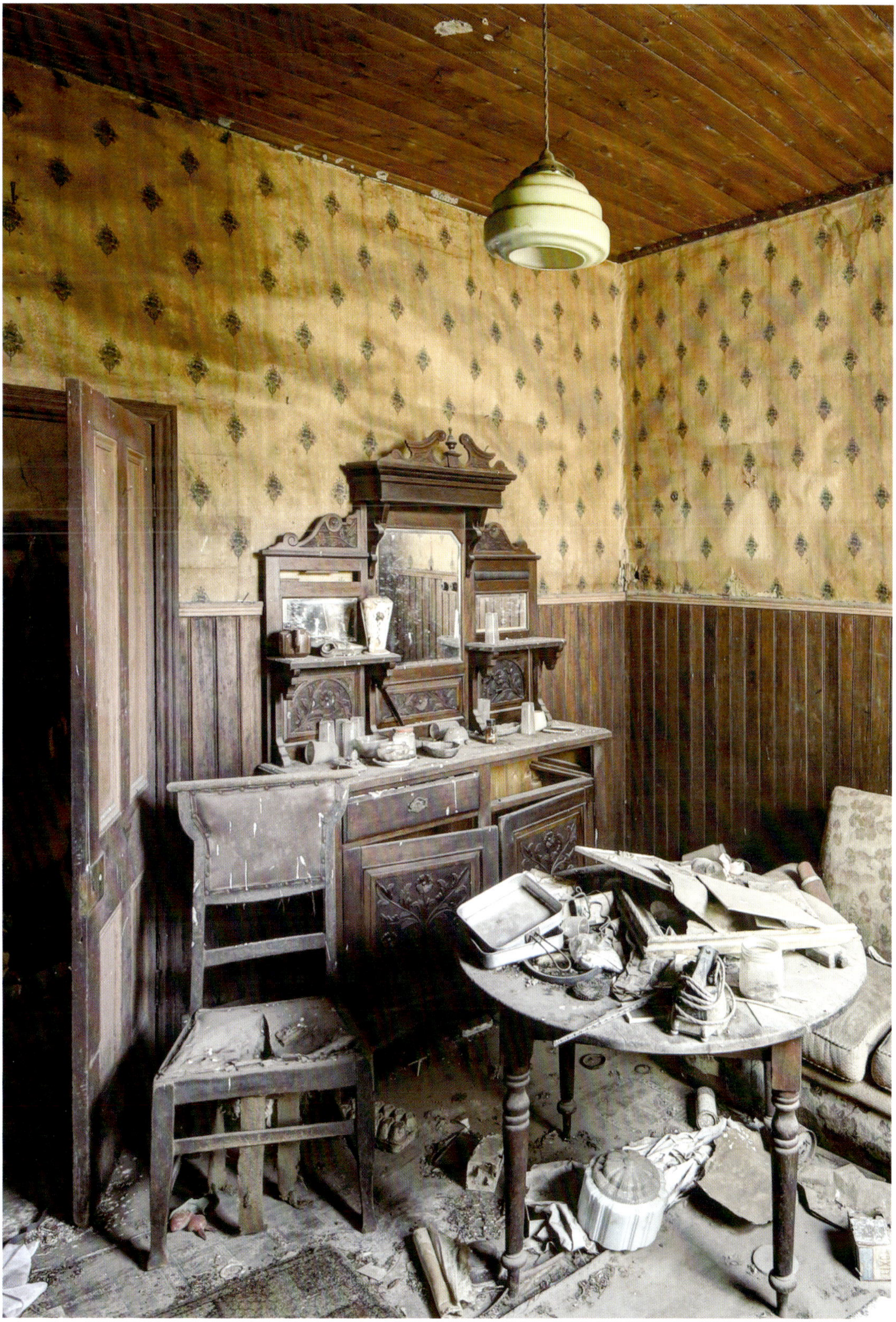

A former dining room still holds its original furniture, with household objects strewn across the table—an eerie tableau of domestic life abruptly abandoned.

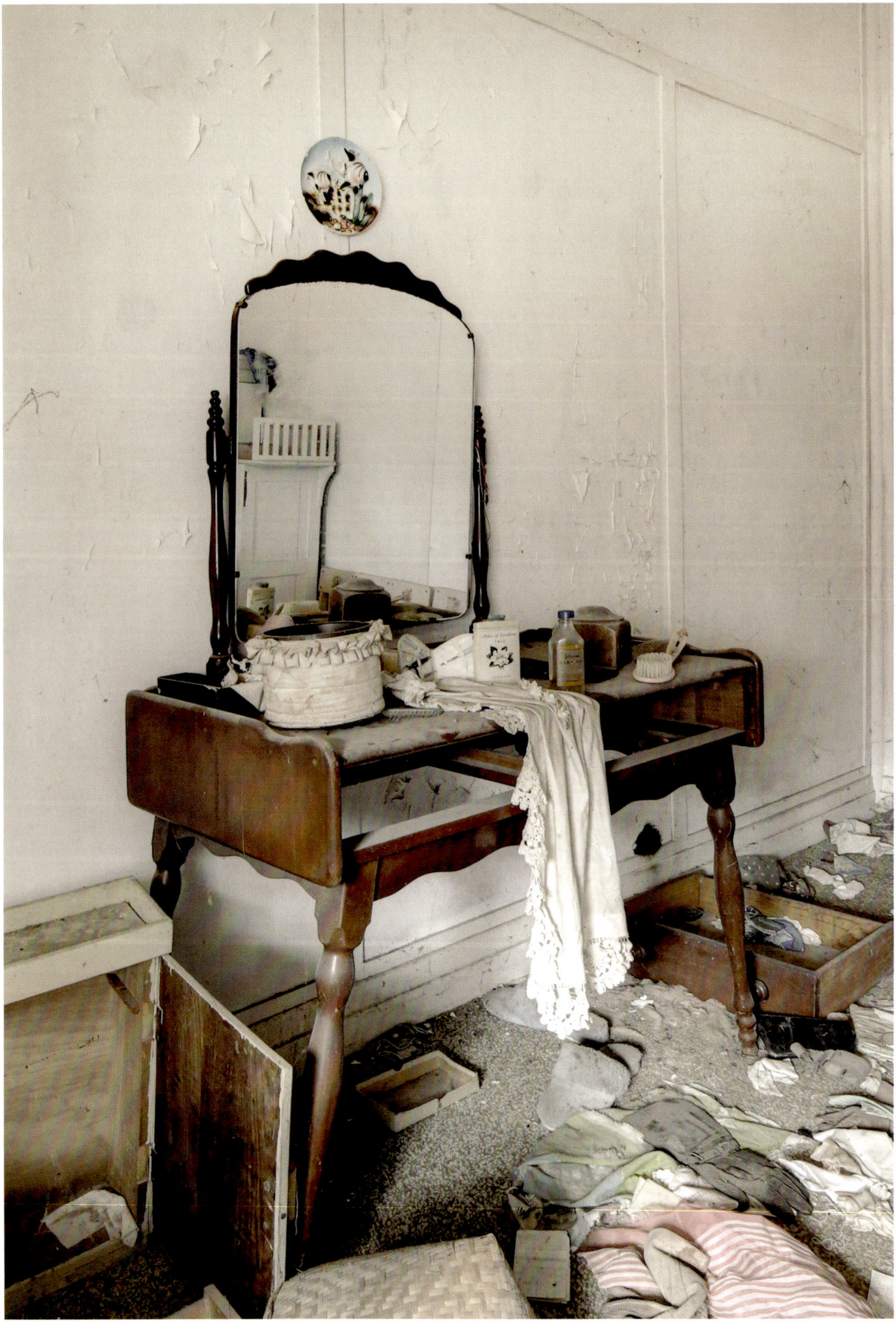

A dusty dressing table stands undisturbed, its surface still lined with original grooming items—quietly echoing the routines of someone long gone.

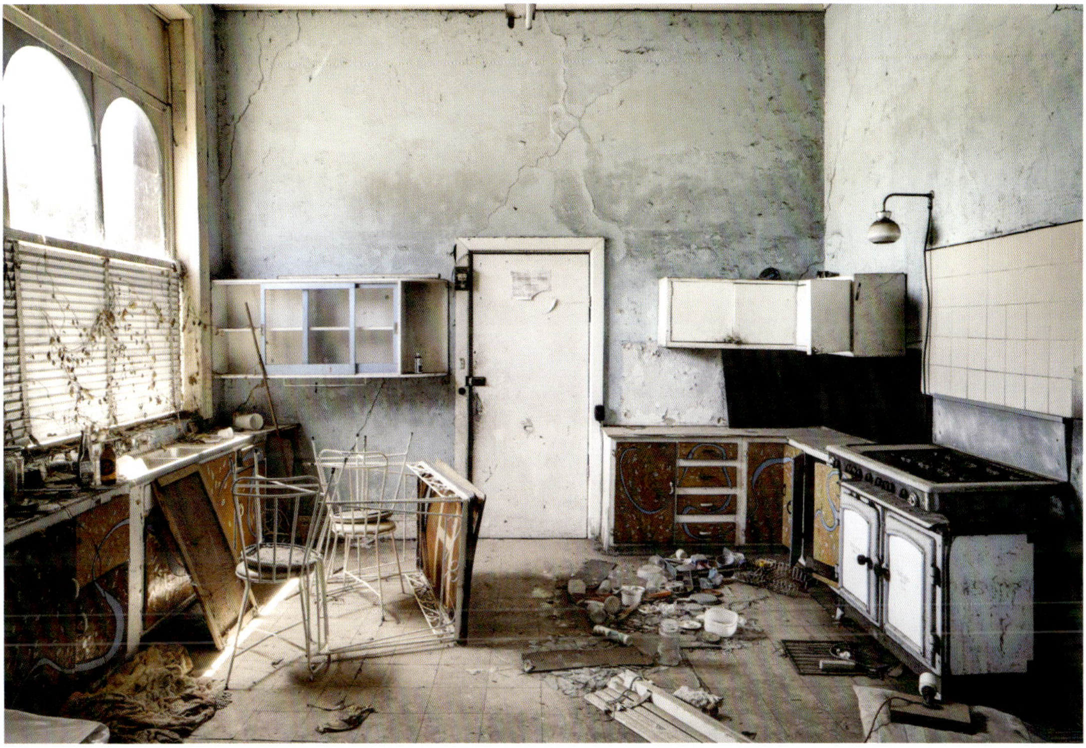

This blue kitchen had a surreal, almost dream-like atmosphere—its soft hues and stillness casting the space in a haze of nostalgia and quiet abandonment.

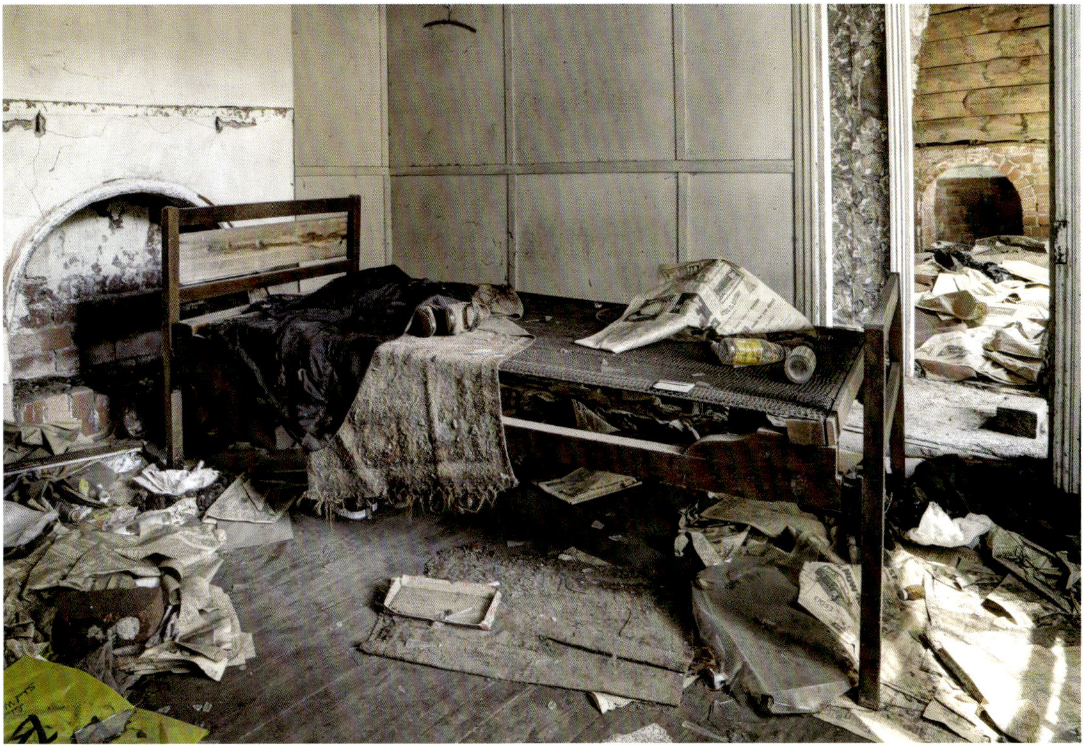

A bed frame stands alone inside this farmhouse, untouched for years—its silence heavy with the weight of time and absence.

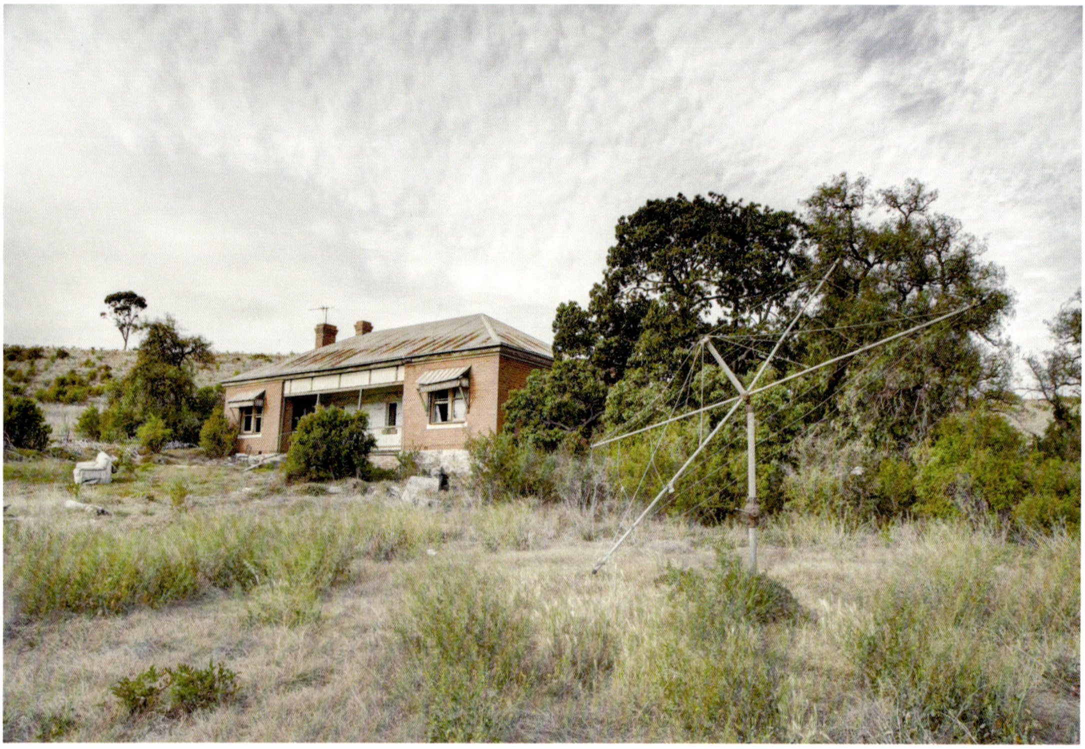

This country homestead featured an original Hills Hoist clothesline—a quintessential element of mid- 20th century Australian life, once spinning with laundry beneath the wide open sky.

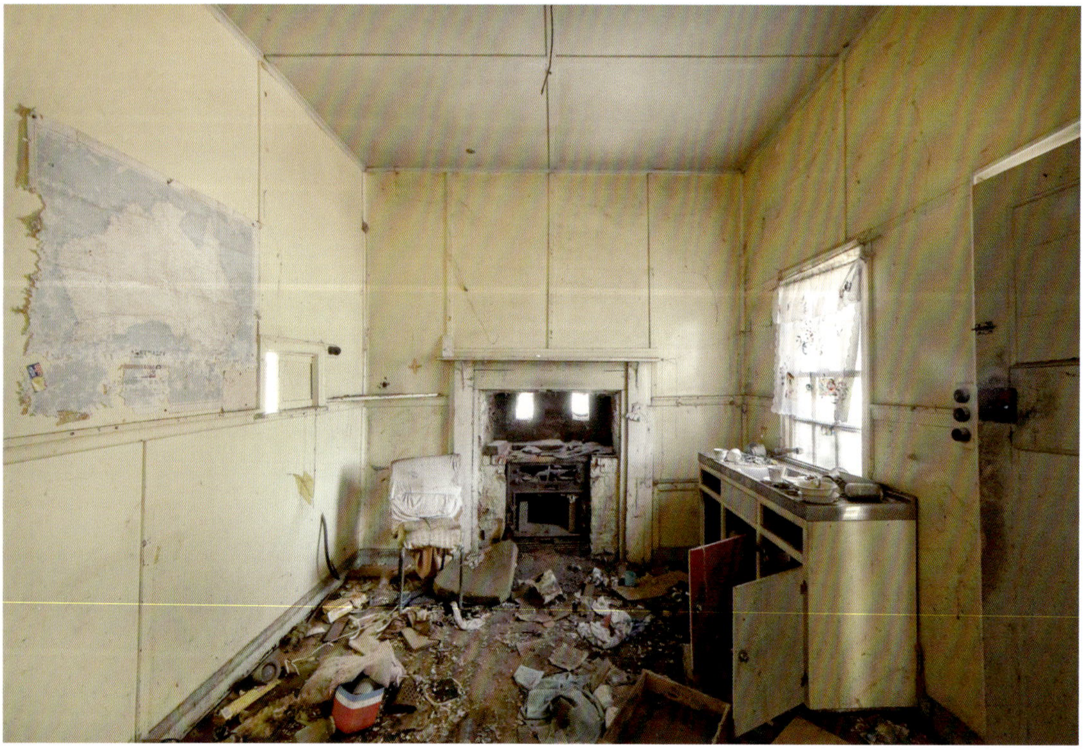

This charming kitchen featured a map of Australia on the wall, marked with a line indicating places visited or dreamed of. This personal detail brought an emotional warmth to the space.

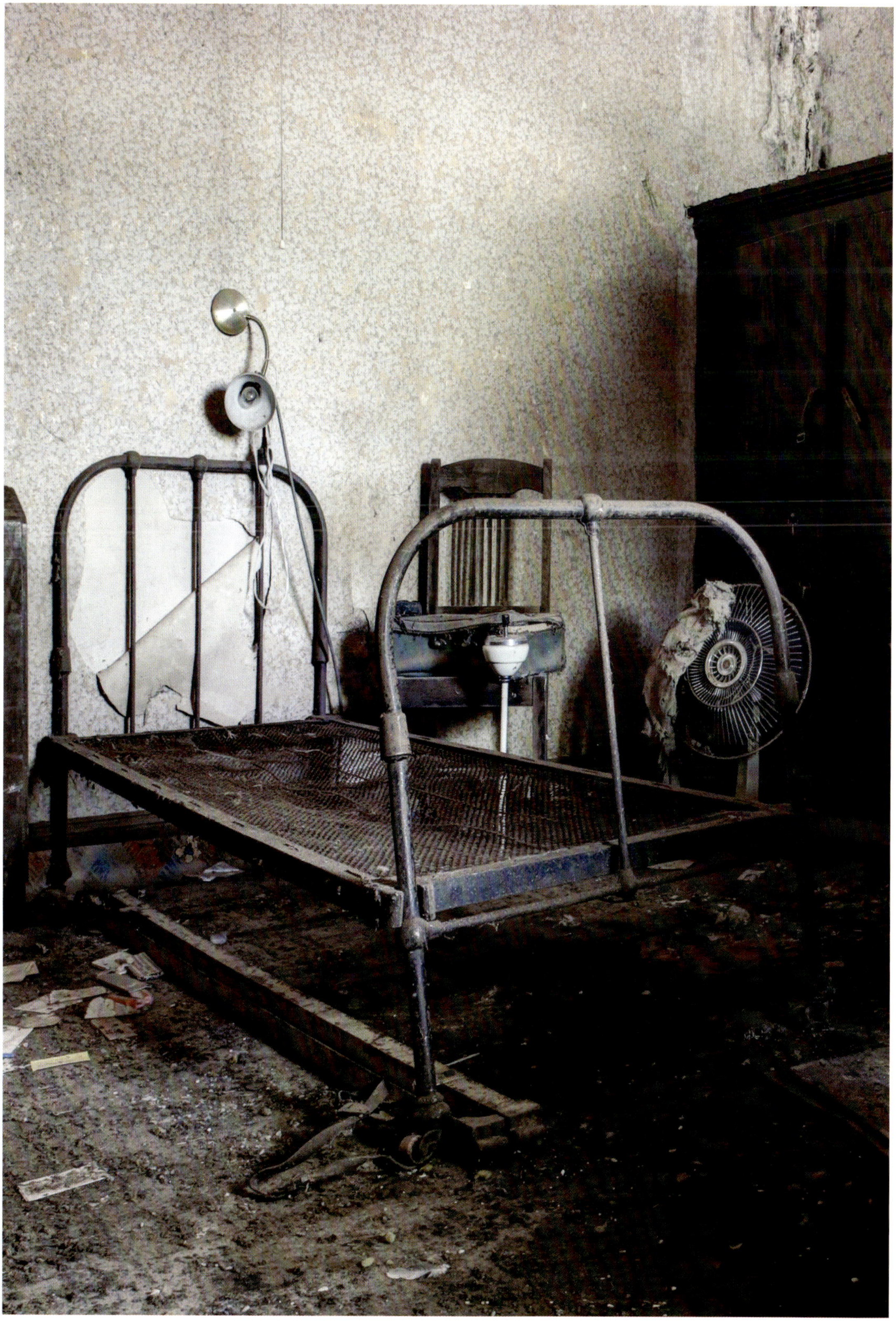

This vintage metal bed frame stood quietly in a darkened room, untouched for years and surrounded by original fixtures that told stories of the past.

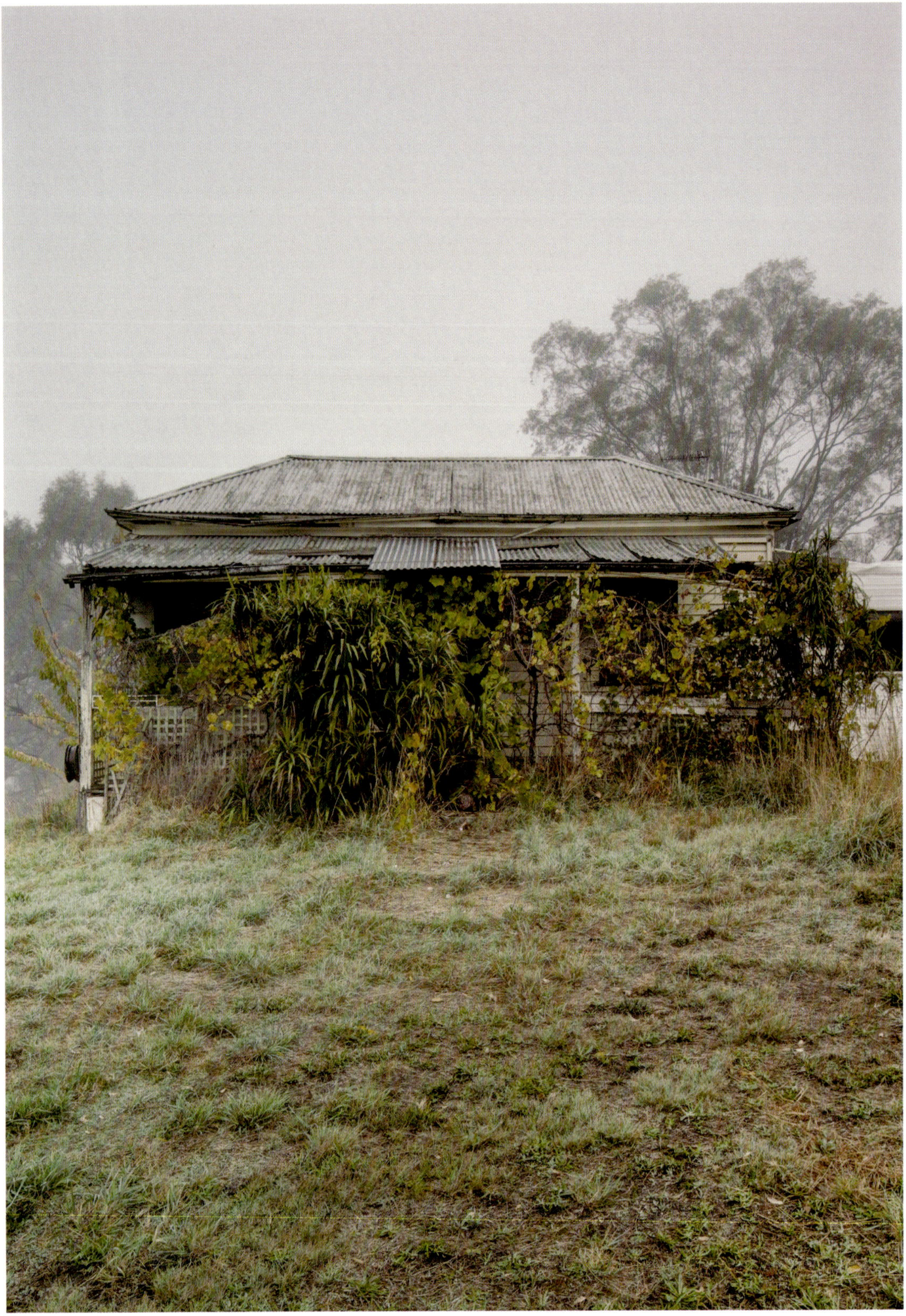

Perched atop a hill in the notorious Central Victorian township of Bonnie Doon—as famously featured in the cult movie 'The Castle'—this weathered shack was overtaken by shrubs and plants, serving as a cozy home for a family of possums nestled in its roof. It has since been demolished.

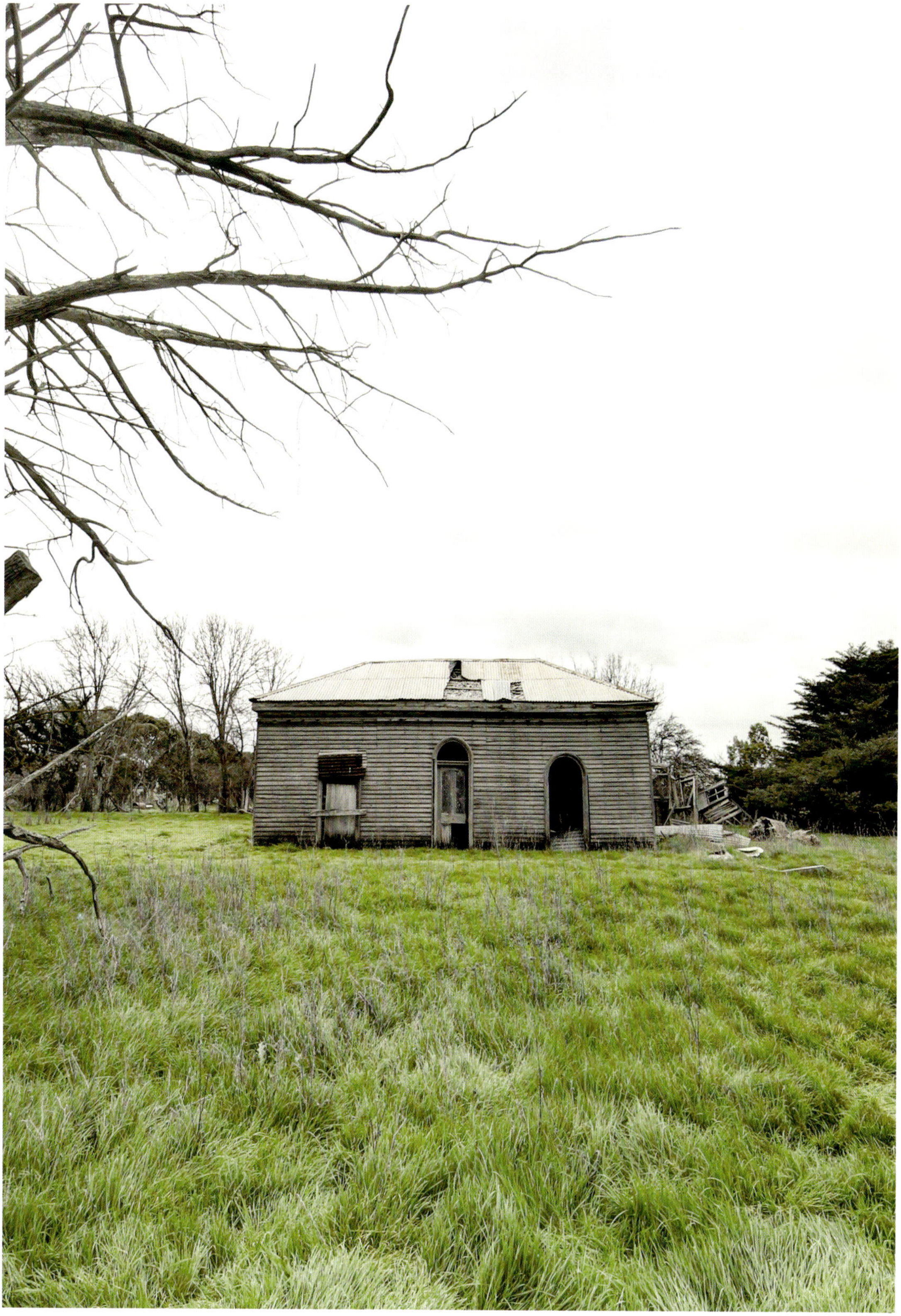

This country shack exuded a mysterious, almost 'witchy' atmosphere, perfectly suited to a cold, misty winter's day in rural Victoria.

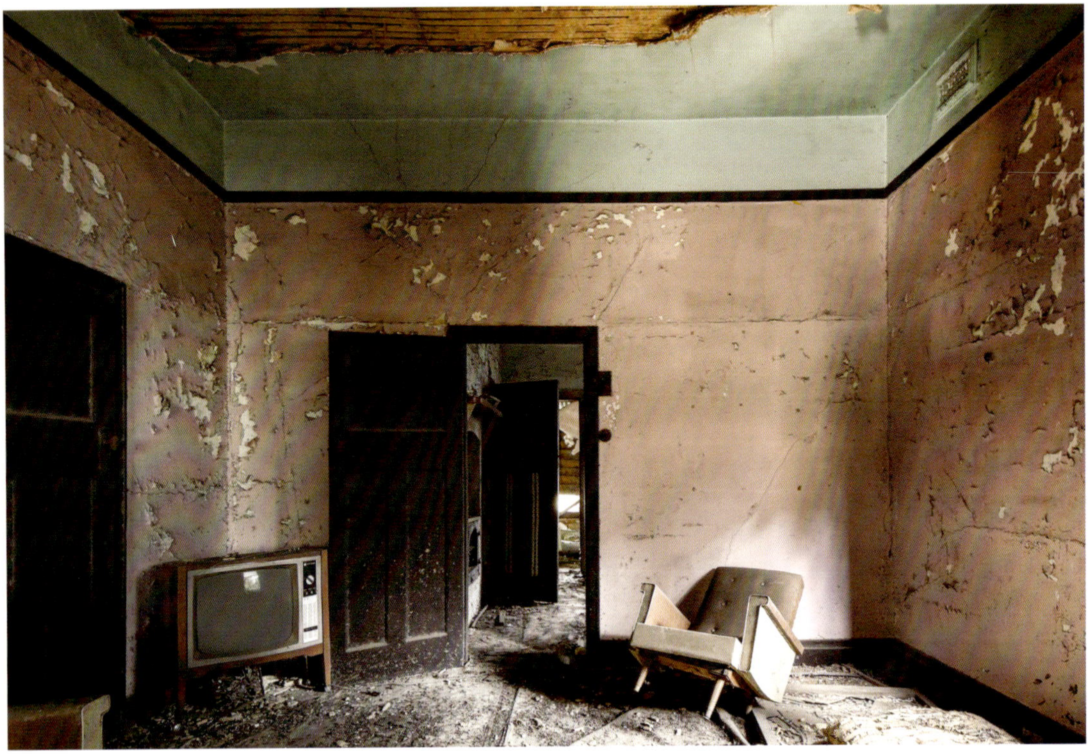

The walls of this wartime-era home were painted in the soft pastel tones typical of the period. Remarkably, it still housed its original lounge furniture and television set.

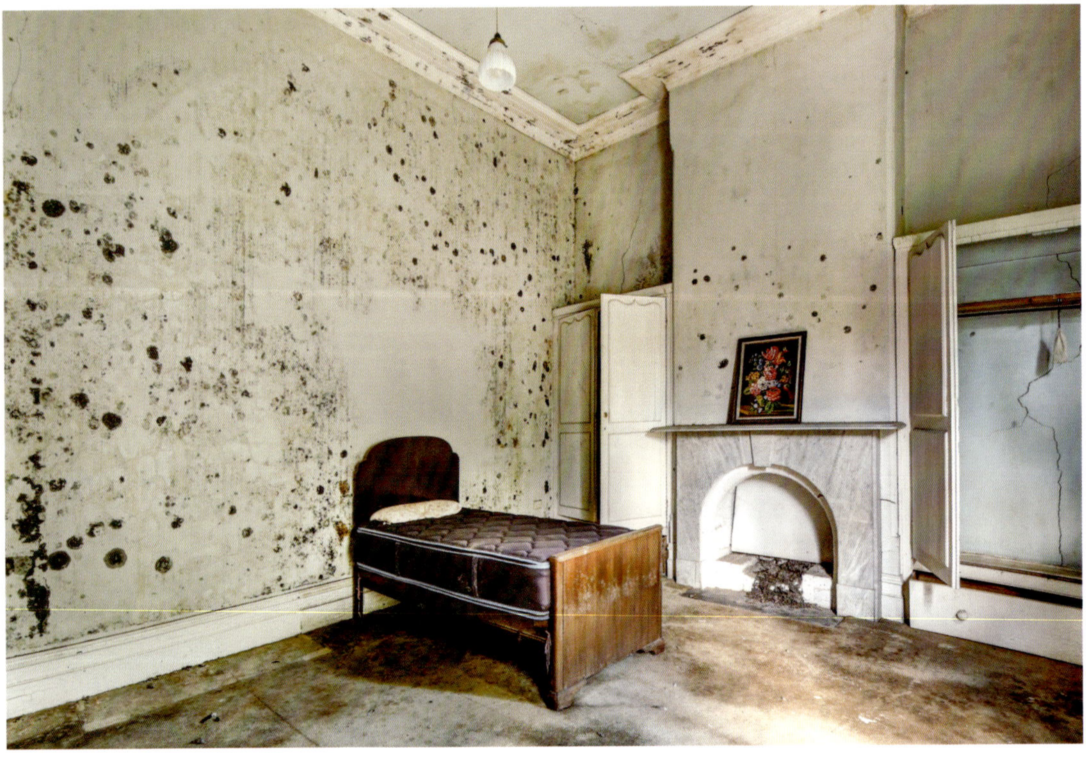

Black mould claims the walls around a lone bed in this derelict inner-city residence.

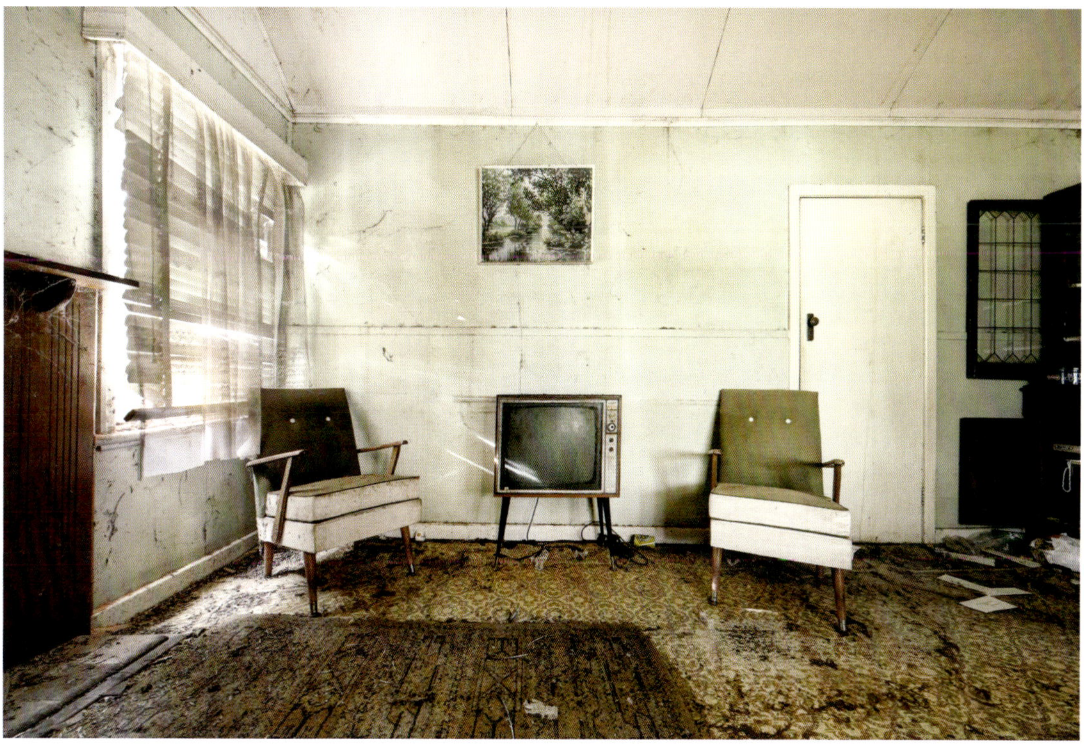

This vintage lounge room remained virtually untouched.

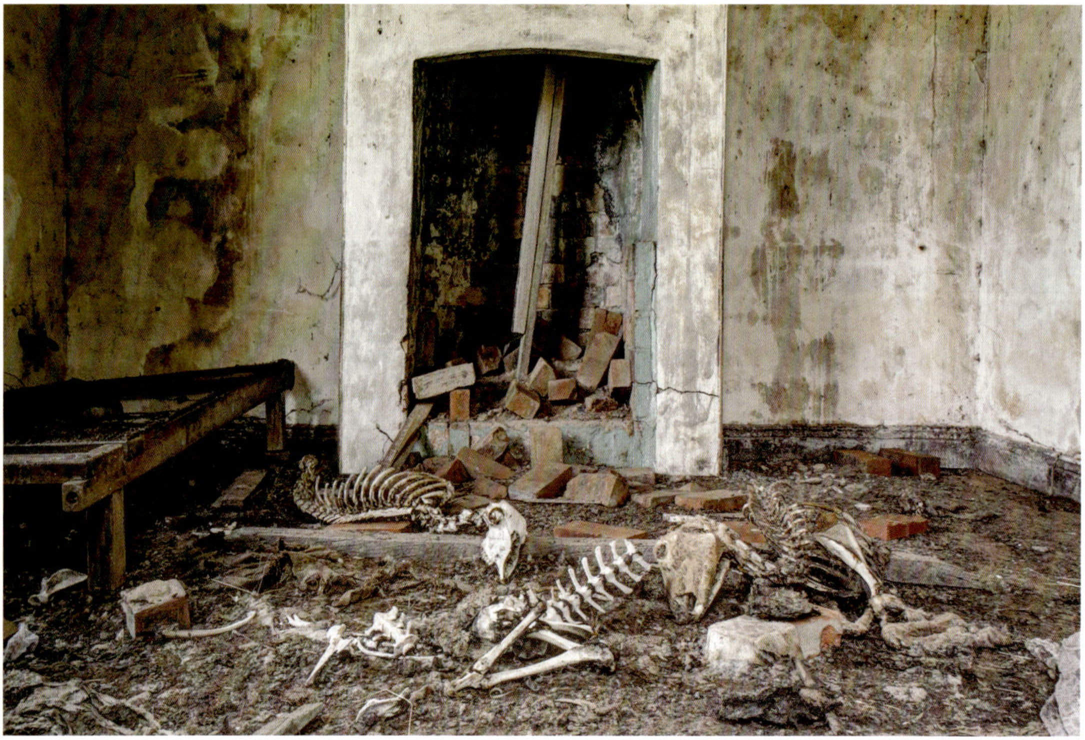

Above and opposite: Many farmers repurpose old homesteads in paddocks as temporary shelters for the remains of livestock.

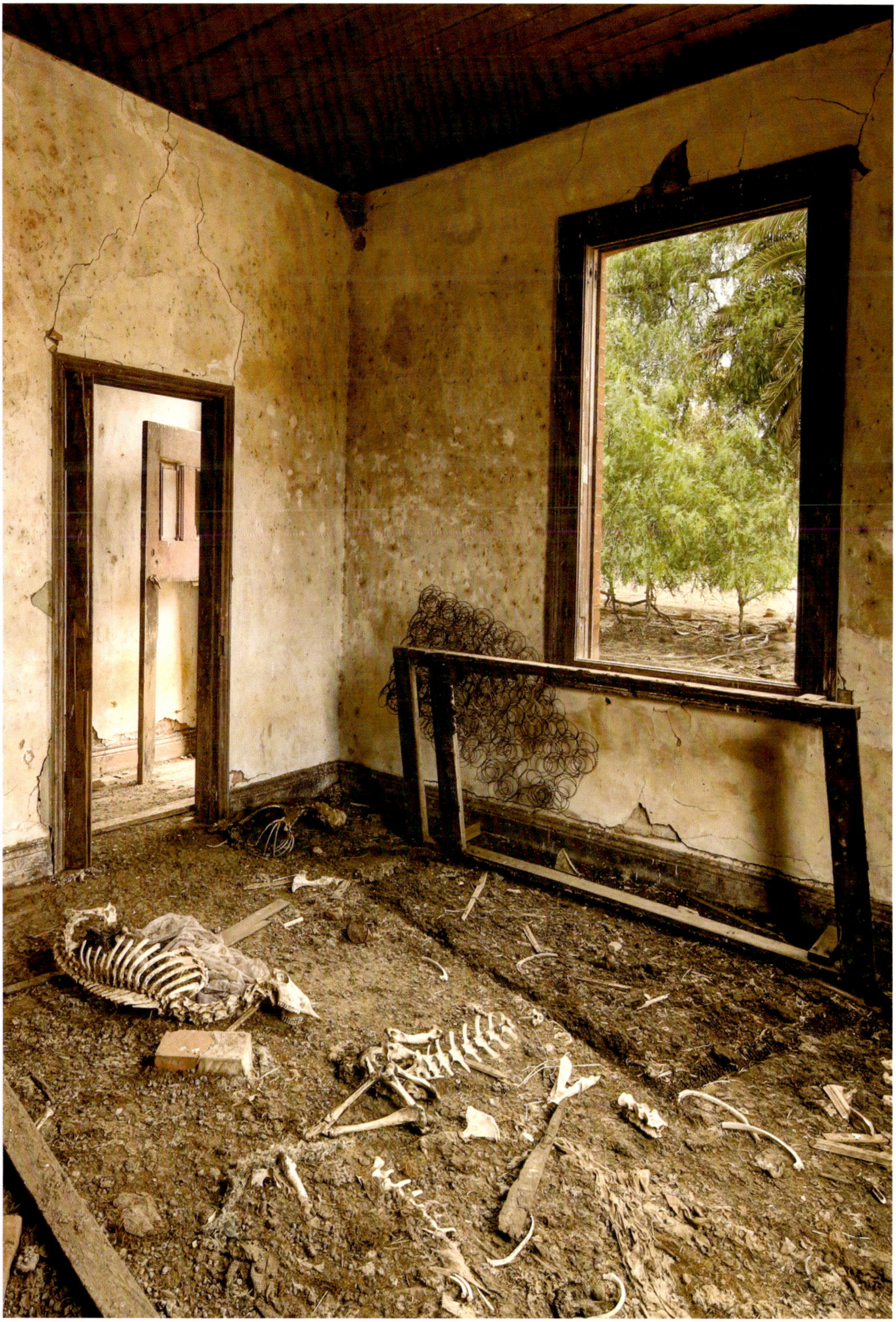

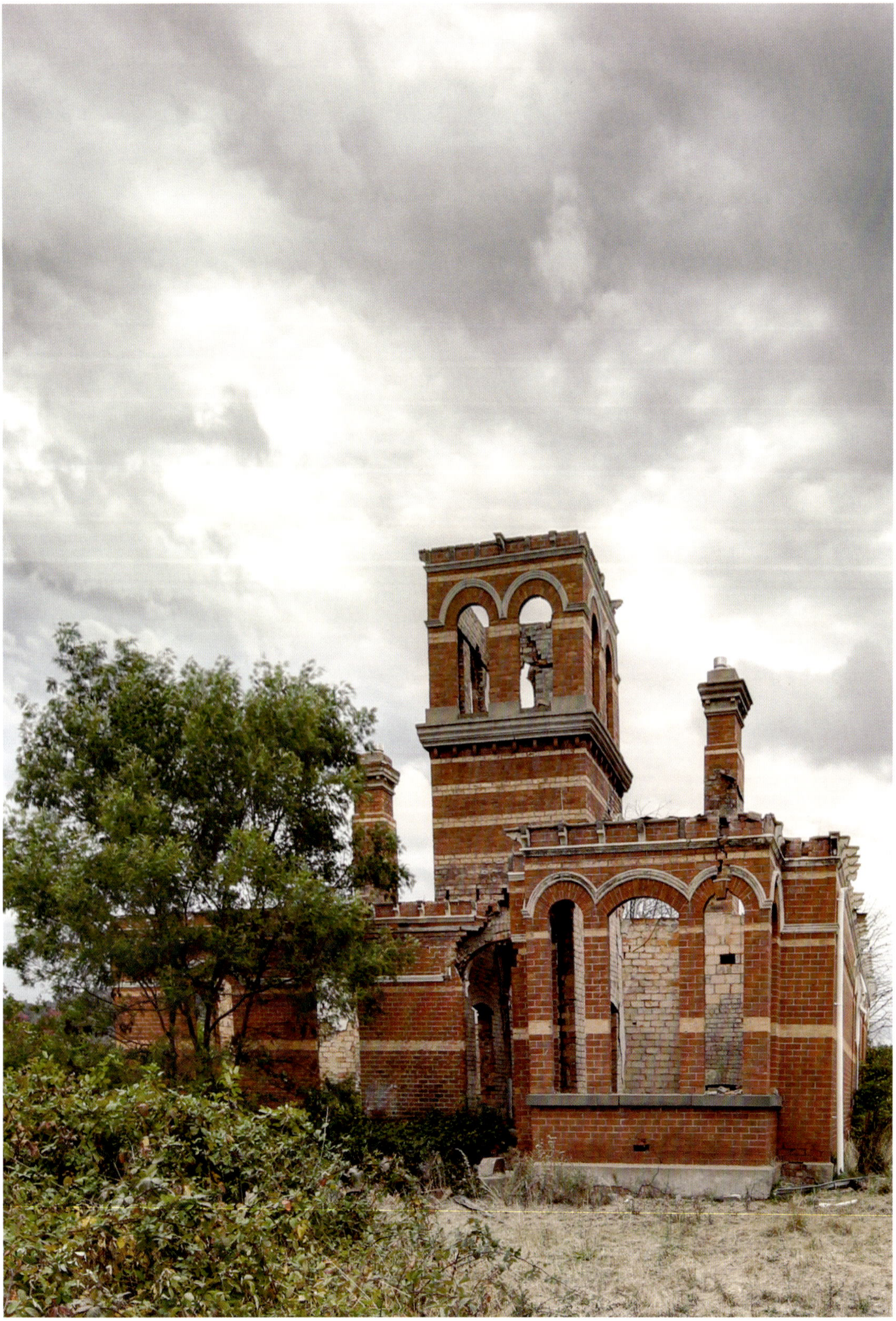

The skeletal remains of this once-grand 19th-century farmhouse have crumbled into little more than a mound of bricks scattered across the ground.

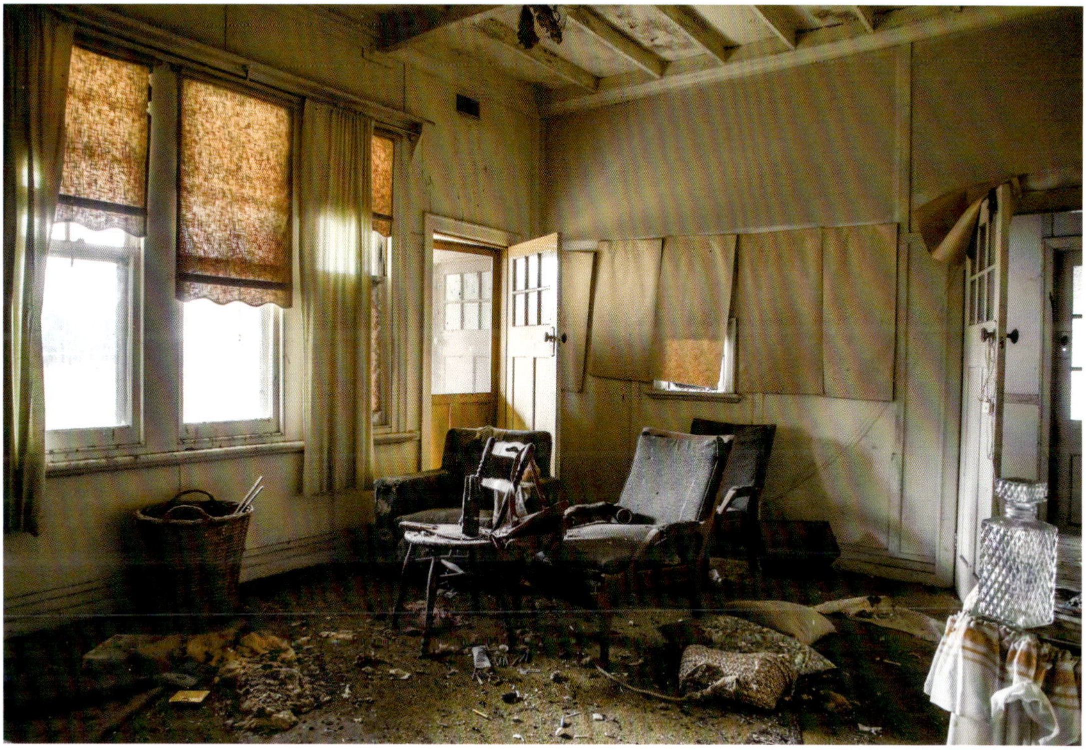

A sunroom—once a relaxed spot for quiet afternoon gatherings.

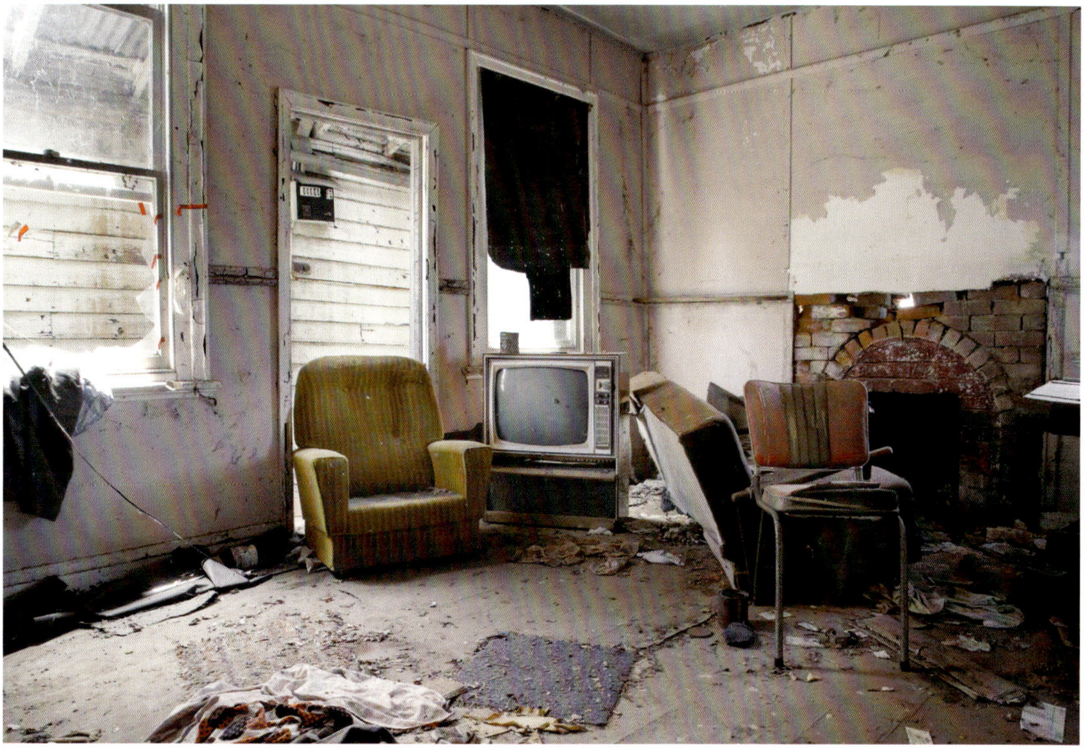

A former lounge room with original fittings and furniture, its walls still painted in the soft pastel hues typical of the wartime era.

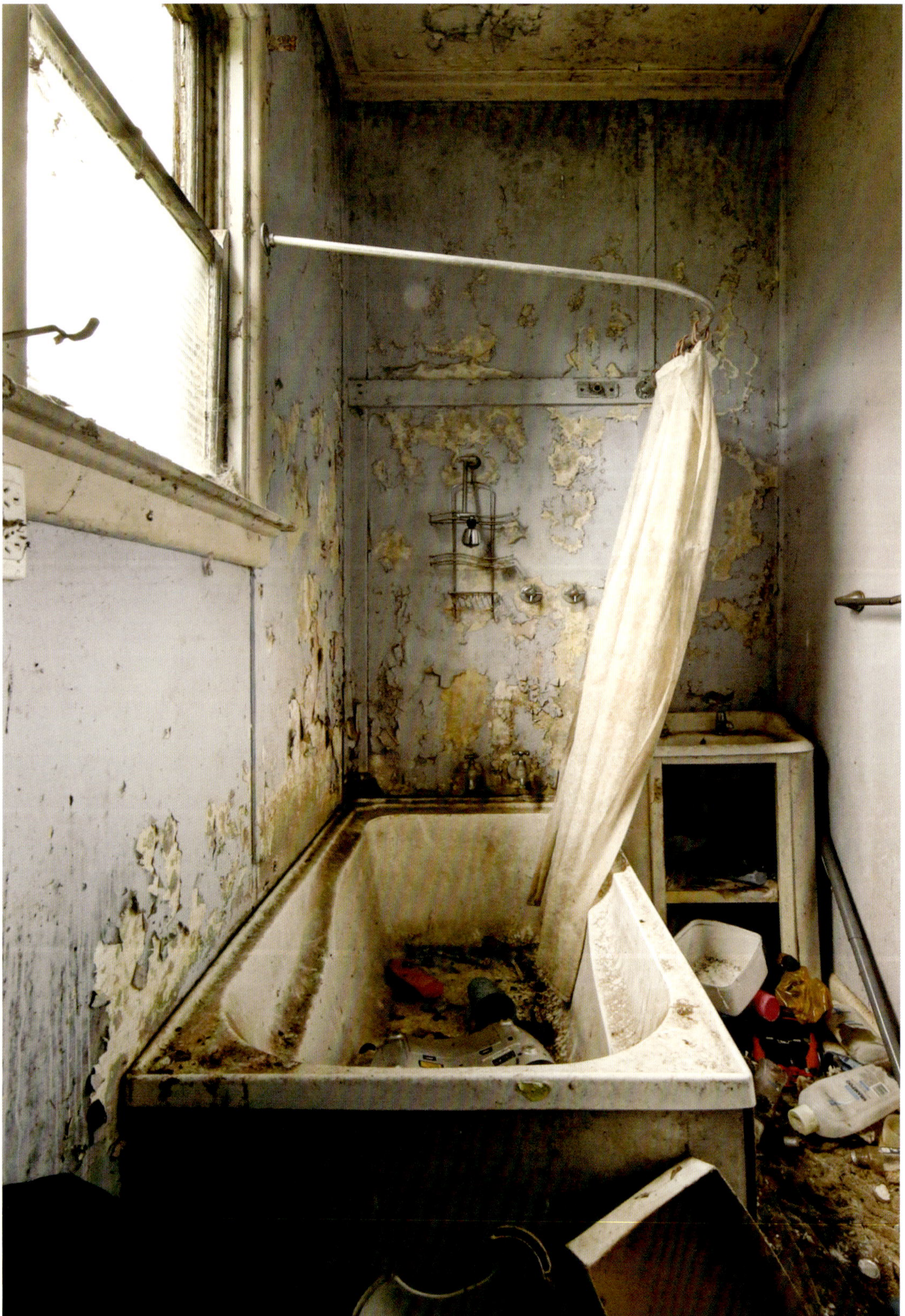

This cottage had the eerie appearance of a cabin straight out of a horror movie, with its weathered exterior and unsettling atmosphere.

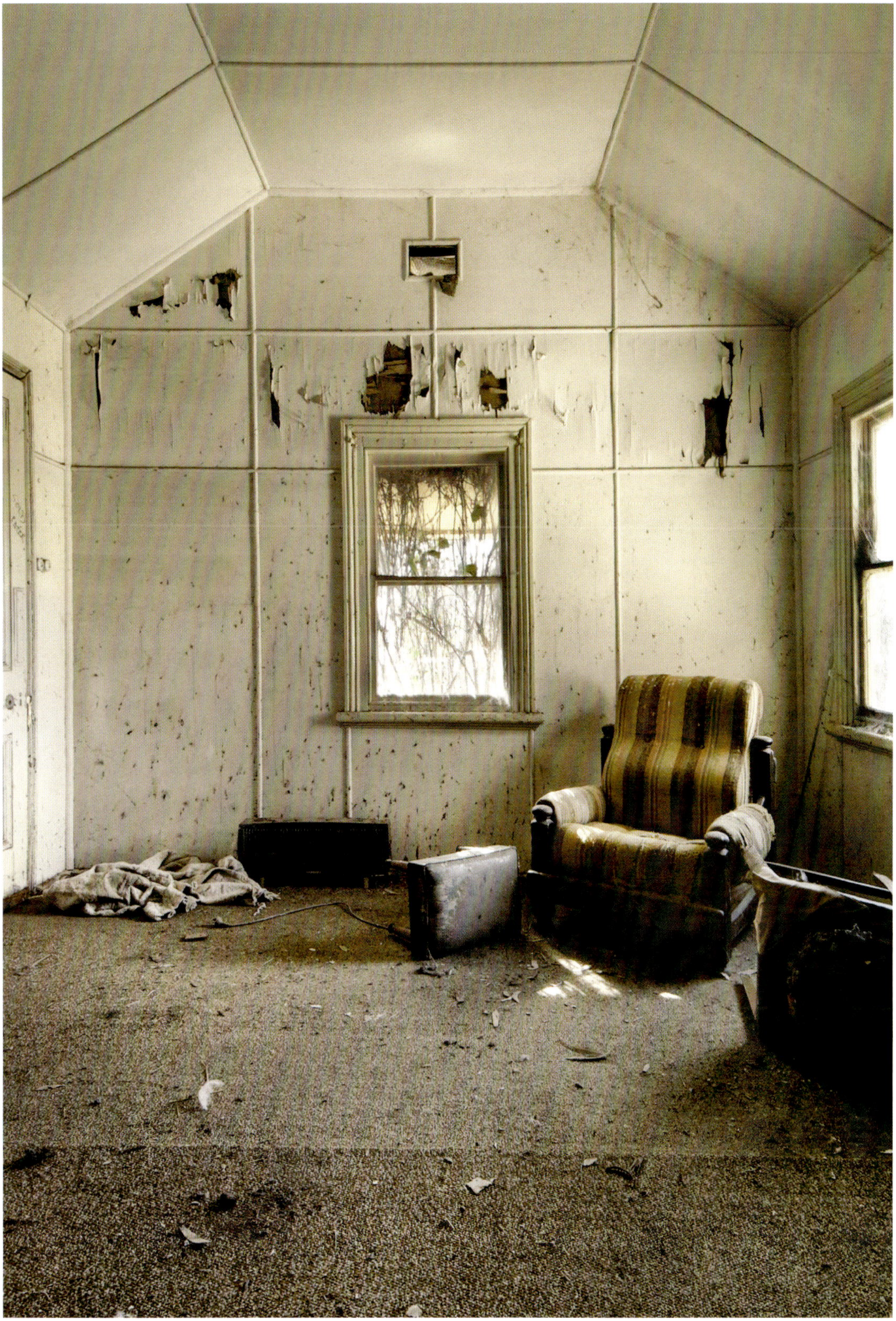

This weathered, wasp infested farmhouse interior has remained untouched for many years.

BENDIGO GASWORKS

Established in the late 1800s by the Bendigo Gas Company, the former Bendigo Gas Works operated continuously until the advent of natural gas in the later 20th century. Over its long history, the site expanded significantly, though it eventually faced challenges brought on by declining gas consumption and rising operational costs.

Major upgrades were undertaken in the early to mid-20th century, with further modernisation following its acquisition by the Gas and Fuel Corporation. Today, the site holds both architectural and historical significance, serving as a rare and tangible link to Victoria's industrial and energy heritage.

One of the site's most striking features is its intricate wall of rusted pipes—twisting and weaving downwards like an industrial waterfall. For photographers and history enthusiasts alike, this complex network of corroded metal offers both a hauntingly beautiful visual composition and a compelling glimpse into the engineering practices of a bygone era.

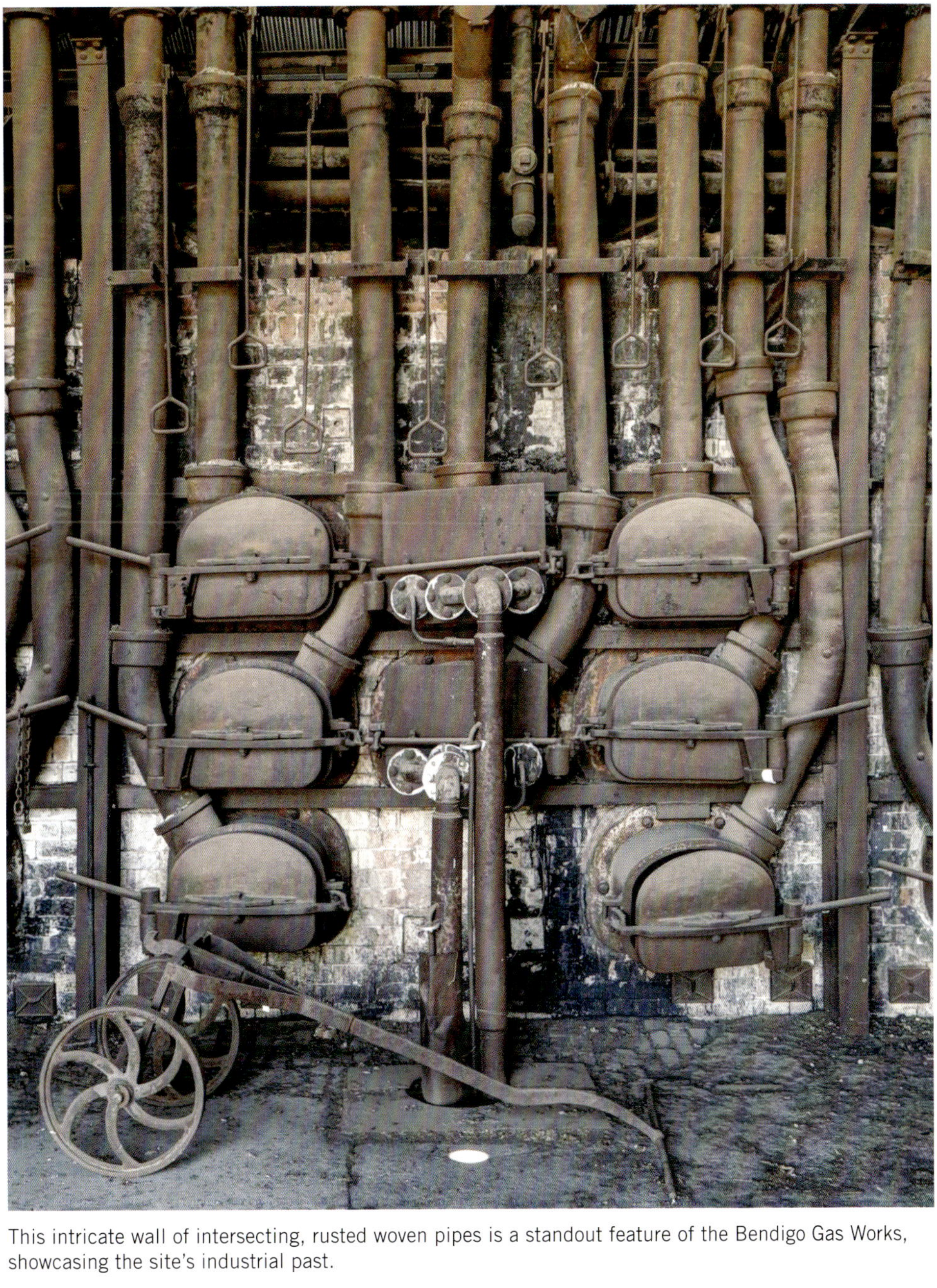

This intricate wall of intersecting, rusted woven pipes is a standout feature of the Bendigo Gas Works, showcasing the site's industrial past.

GEELONG POWER PLANT

Positioned on Geelong's waterfront, this imposing structure once embodied the spirit of post-war industrial ambition. Opened in the mid-20th century, it was the largest power facility in Victoria outside the Latrobe Valley, constructed to meet the escalating electricity demands of Geelong's expanding industries and population.

As more efficient power stations were commissioned across Victoria, the plant's role steadily declined. By the 1960s, it was used only during periods of peak demand due to its high operating costs. The commissioning of newer facilities eventually rendered it obsolete, and it was officially decommissioned in the 1970s. Despite its closure, the imposing structure remains a prominent landmark within Geelong's industrial landscape.

In the decades since, the decommissioned power station has taken on a new life as a creative sanctuary. Artists, photographers and filmmakers have gravitated to the site, drawn by its towering industrial forms, textured decay and dramatic light. The raw, cavernous interiors and echoes of machinery now serve as an evocative backdrop for visual storytelling and experimental projects. No longer producing electricity, the power plant continues to generate inspiration—proof that even the most utilitarian of structures can find new meaning through artistic reinvention.

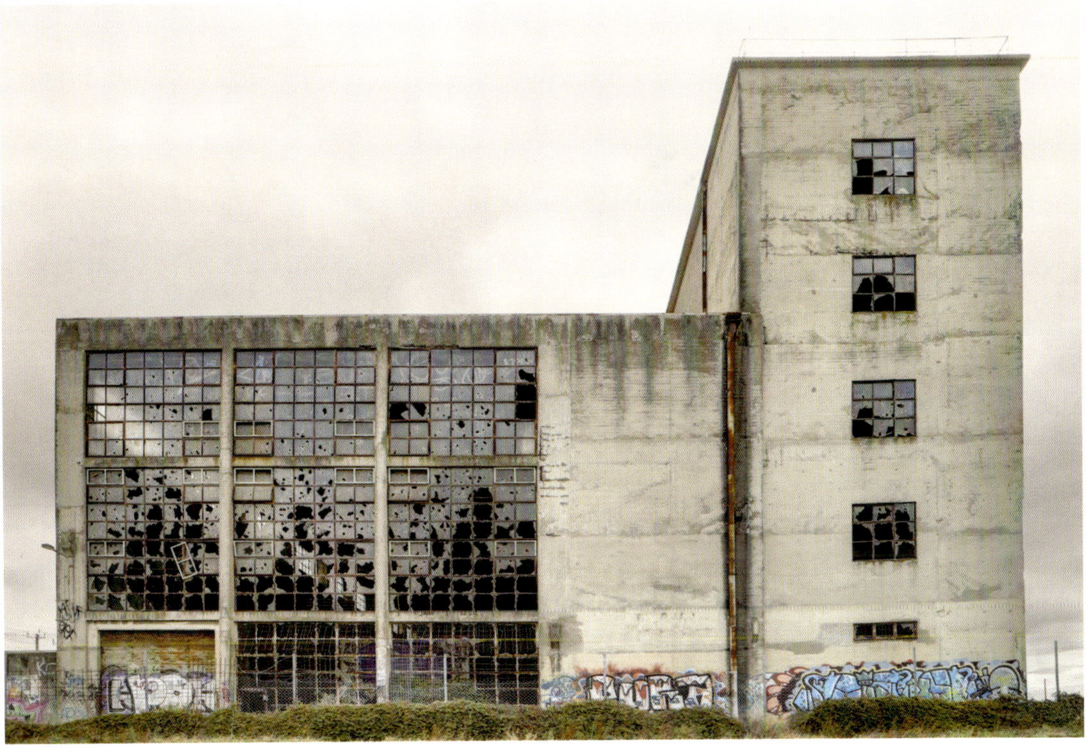

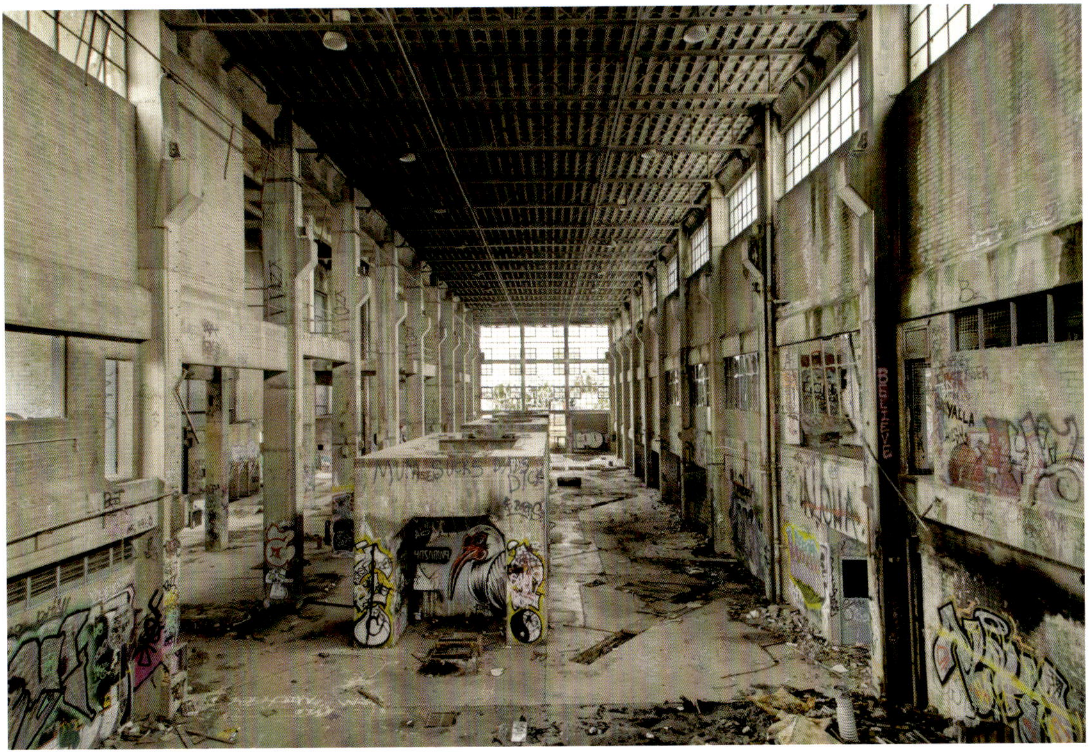

Above and below: The long-abandoned Geelong power plant has become a haven for street artists, offering a vast, gritty canvas where they can freely practise and showcase their craft.

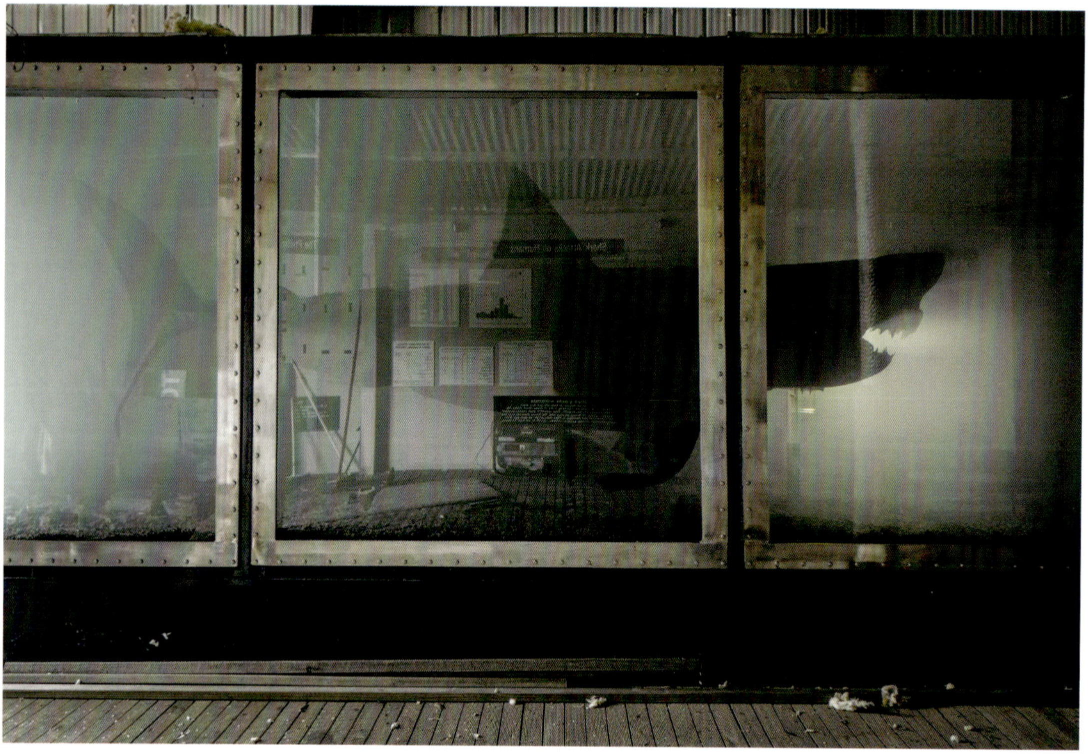

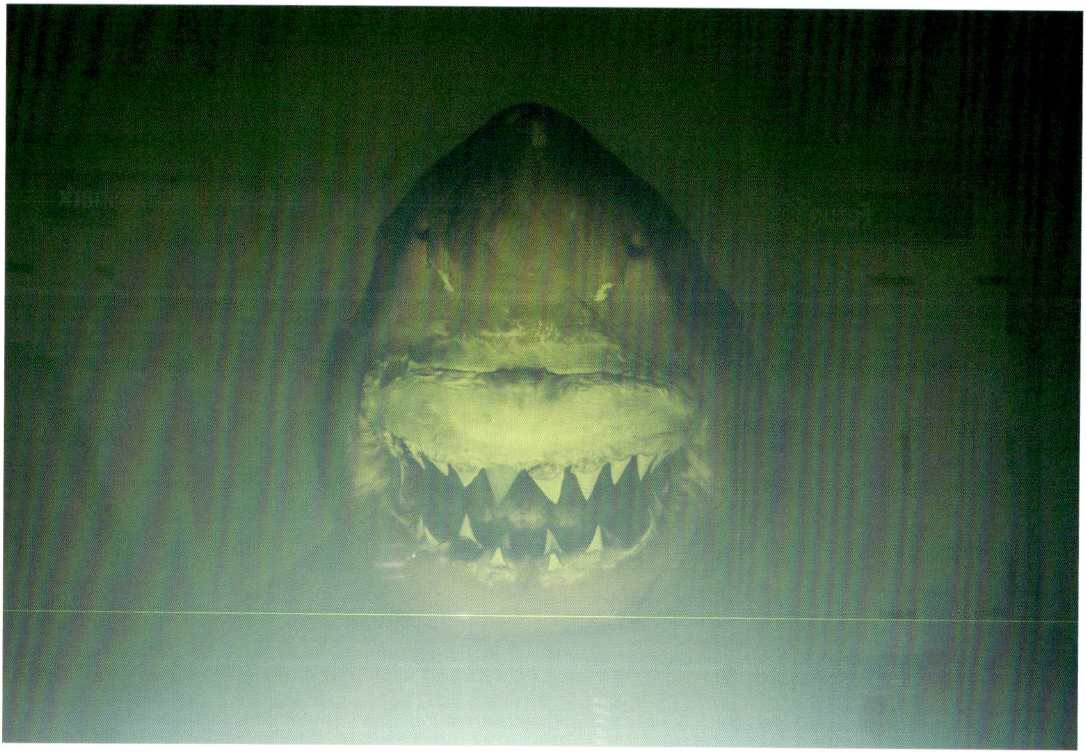

Above and below: This preserved great white shark at Wildlife Wonderland was left floating in a darkened tank for years. In 2019, it was finally relocated to a new home at an exhibition centre.

WILDLIFE WONDERLAND

Wildlife Wonderland, in Bass, was once a popular tourist attraction that showcased native Australian wildlife. Opened in the 1980s, the park featured a variety of animals, including koalas, kangaroos, emus plus more exotic species, offering visitors a chance to learn about and interact with Australia's unique fauna. The park was particularly known for its educational programs and conservation efforts.

However, as time passed, the park faced financial difficulties and declining visitor numbers. Despite attempts at revitalisation, Wildlife Wonderland ultimately closed its doors. The site was abandoned, and the once-thriving park fell into disrepair.

In the years following its closure, the spaces deserted grounds became a magnet for urban explorers. Drawn by the eerie stillness, faded signage and remnants of animal enclosures, these visitors documented nature's slow reclamation of the dilapidated site. From the crumbling, infamous giant worm-shaped building to the preserved great white shark still suspended in its tank of formaldehyde, the attraction offered a haunting glimpse into a forgotten world—transforming its remaining structures into a surreal destination for those captivated by decay, abandonment and hidden histories.

THE RED RATTLER

The Red Rattler train carriages, emblematic of Melbourne's public transport history, were once a familiar sight on the city's suburban rail network. Introduced in the early 1900s, these distinctive red carriages were known for their simple design and rickety yet reliable service, often becoming a symbol of Melbourne's early 20th century rail culture.

By the 1980s, Red Rattlers were gradually phased out in favour of more modern trains, and many were retired from service. Some of the abandoned carriages found their way to storage yards and fields, where they were left to deteriorate, becoming a point of interest for urban explorers and photographers.

Today, the abandoned carriages stand as nostalgic reminders of Melbourne's past, symbolising the evolution of the city's rail system and the end of an era in the state's transport history. As Melbourne enters a new phase with the opening of the Metro Tunnel, these historic trains offer a tangible link to the city's rich rail heritage amid the promise of modern innovation.

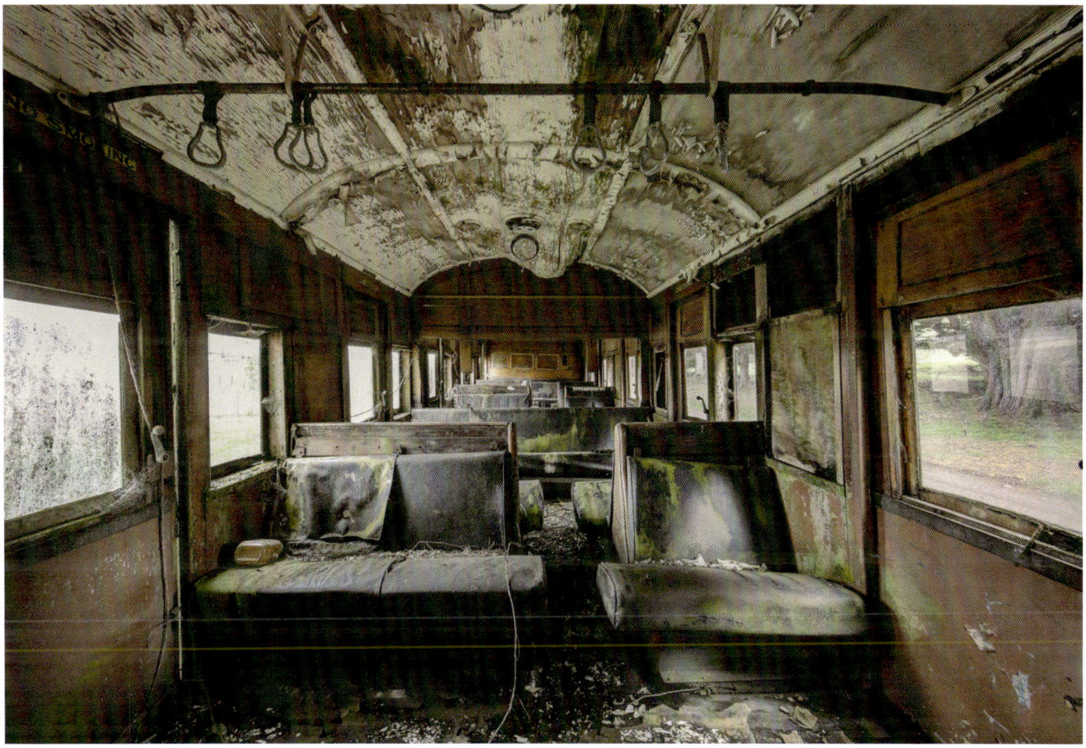

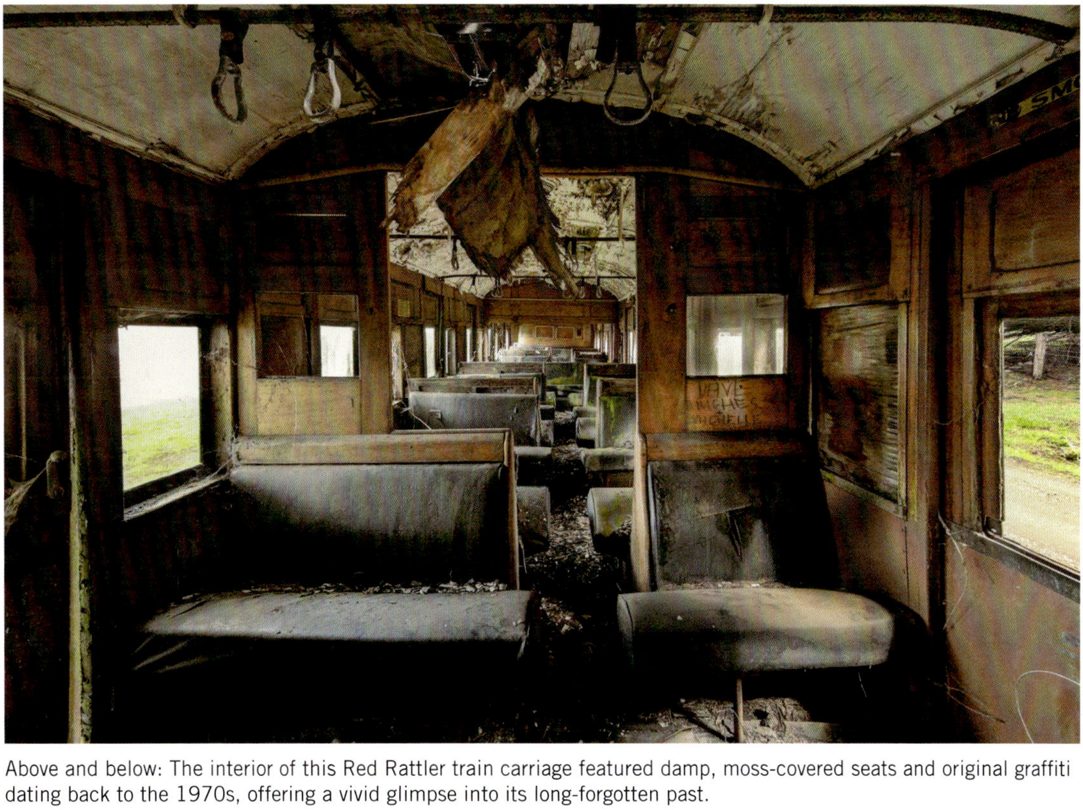

Above and below: The interior of this Red Rattler train carriage featured damp, moss-covered seats and original graffiti dating back to the 1970s, offering a vivid glimpse into its long-forgotten past.

HITACHI TRAINS

Melbourne's Hitachi train carriages, introduced in the early 1970s, were a significant step forward in the modernisation of the city's suburban rail network. Assembled locally, these stainless-steel trains quickly became iconic for their distinctive design—angular bodies, sliding doors and open saloon seating. Although they lacked the comforts of air conditioning, Hitachis represented reliable, no-frills public transport that served millions of commuters across decades.

Operating for over 30 years, the Hitachi fleet became deeply ingrained in Melbourne's daily life. They were renowned for their resilience and simplicity, lacking many of the complex systems that would become standard in later models. While some passengers recall them fondly for their retro charm, others saw them as noisy and outdated by the 2000s. Nevertheless, their durability kept them in service long after their intended retirement, especially during fleet shortages or maintenance periods for newer trains.

Most of the Hitachi units were eventually decommissioned and scrapped, with a few preserved by heritage rail groups. However, not all shared such a dignified fate. One abandoned carriage lies forgotten in a paddock, its frame overtaken by weeds. Standing inside its empty shell, one is struck by a sense of quiet nostalgia—a relic from a time when these carriages made up vital arteries of a busy city. In its decaying form, the carriage offers a haunting yet oddly poetic platform for reflection, not just on Melbourne's transport history, but on the passing of eras and the impermanence of the everyday.

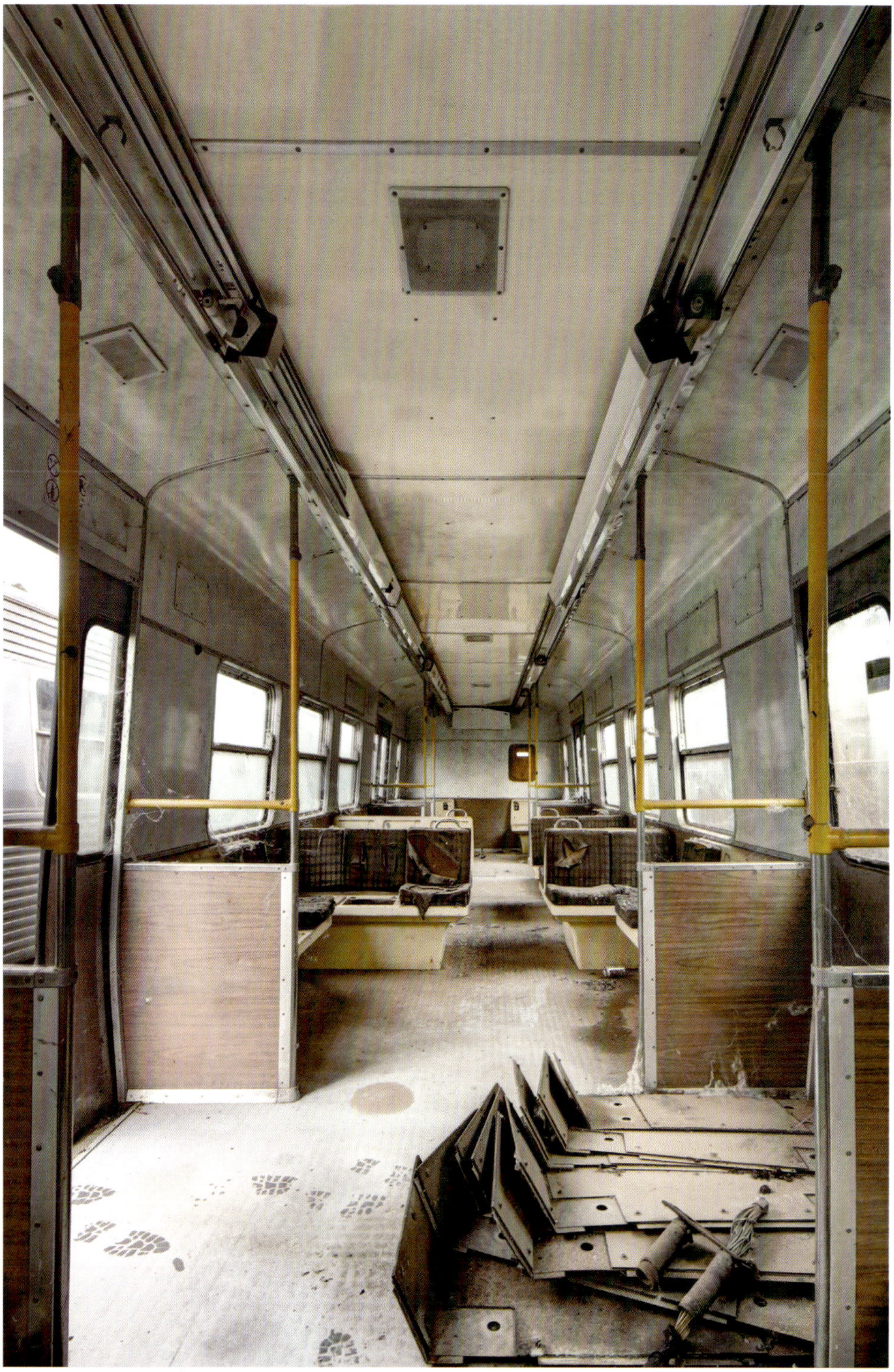

The interior of this Hitachi train carriage evokes strong memories for those who spent years commuting to school or work aboard its familiar compartments.

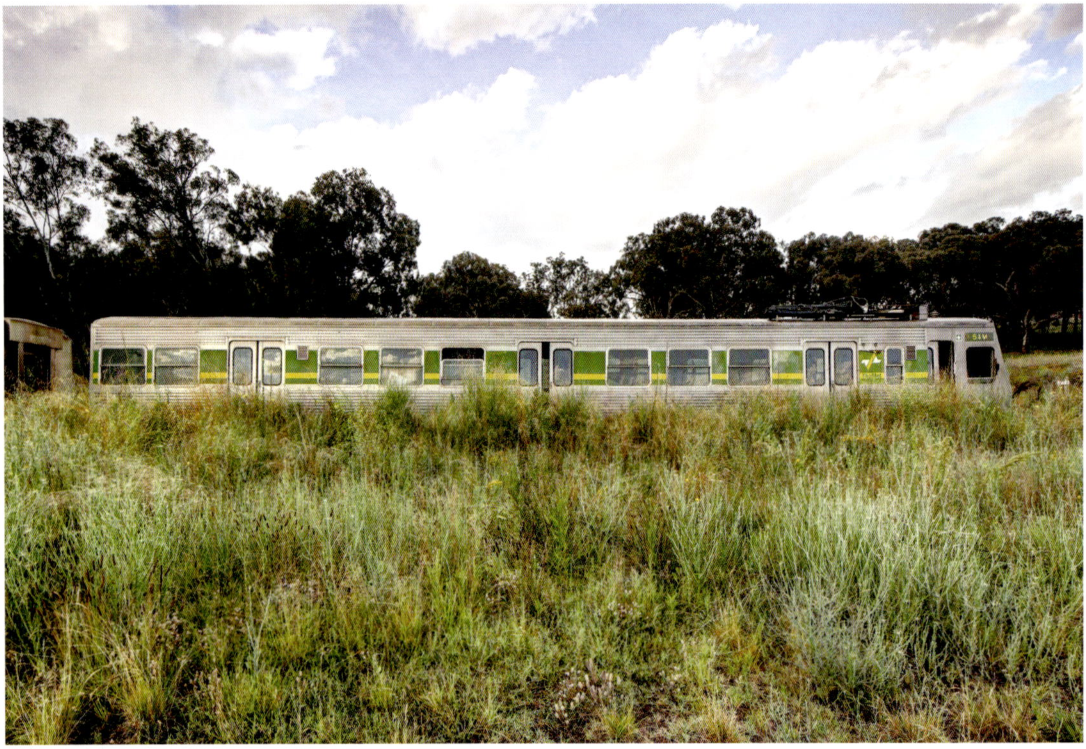

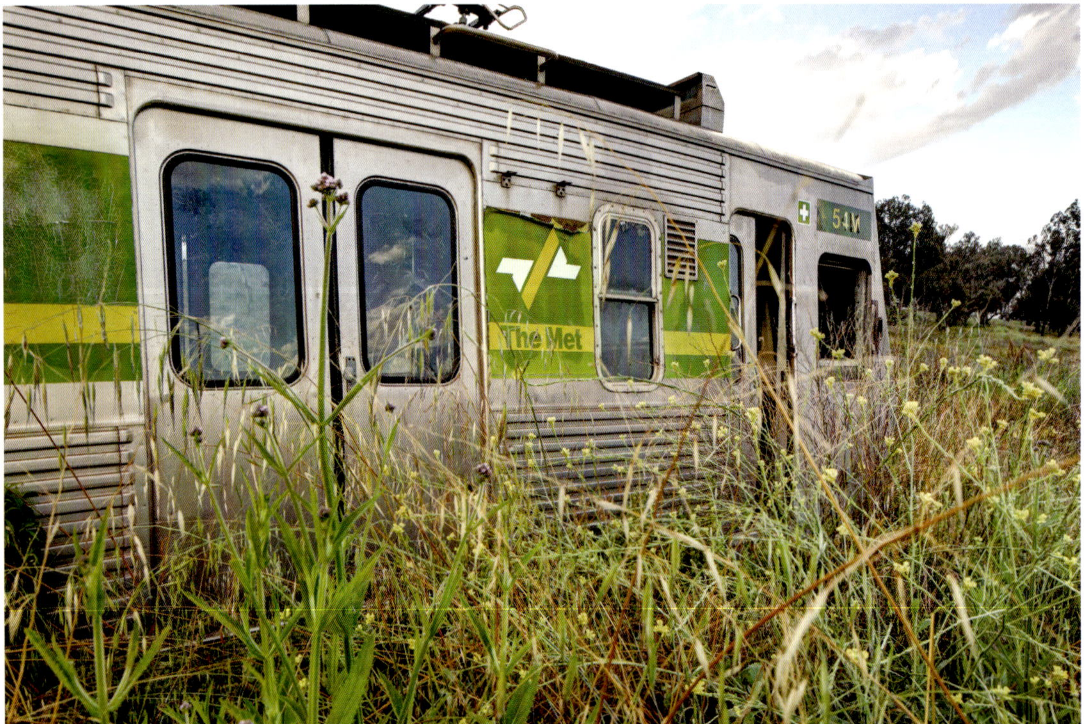

This abandoned train carriage sits forgotten in a field, slowly being swallowed by encroaching grass and weeds.

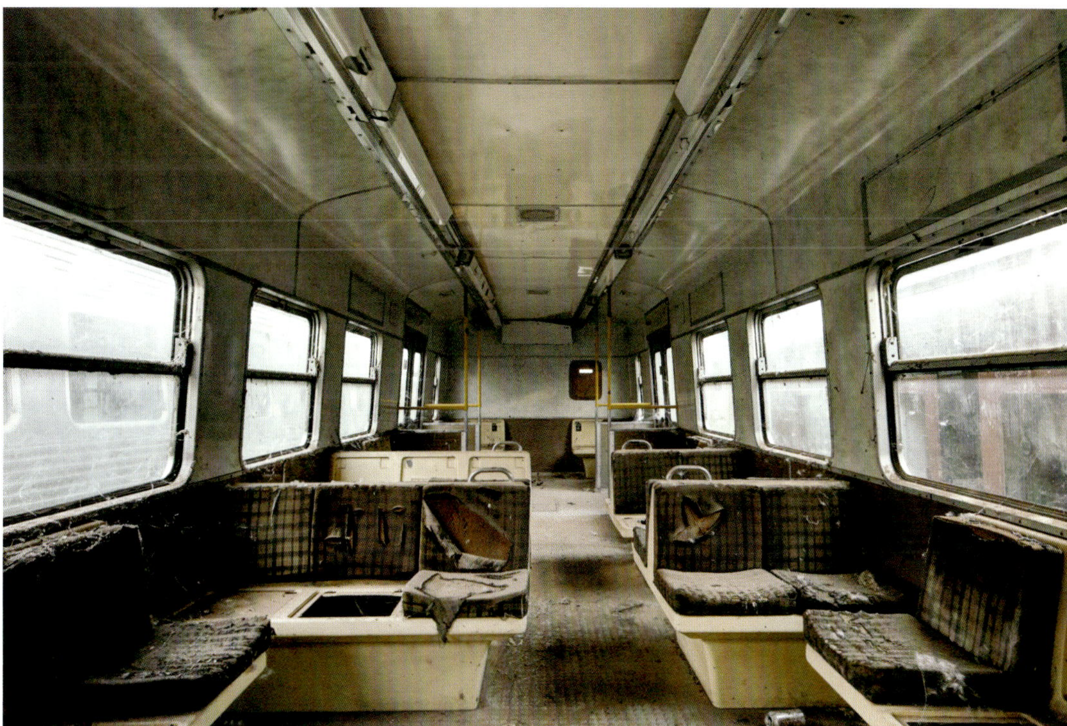

Etched in fabric and memory—the unmistakable seat pattern of every Hitachi commute.

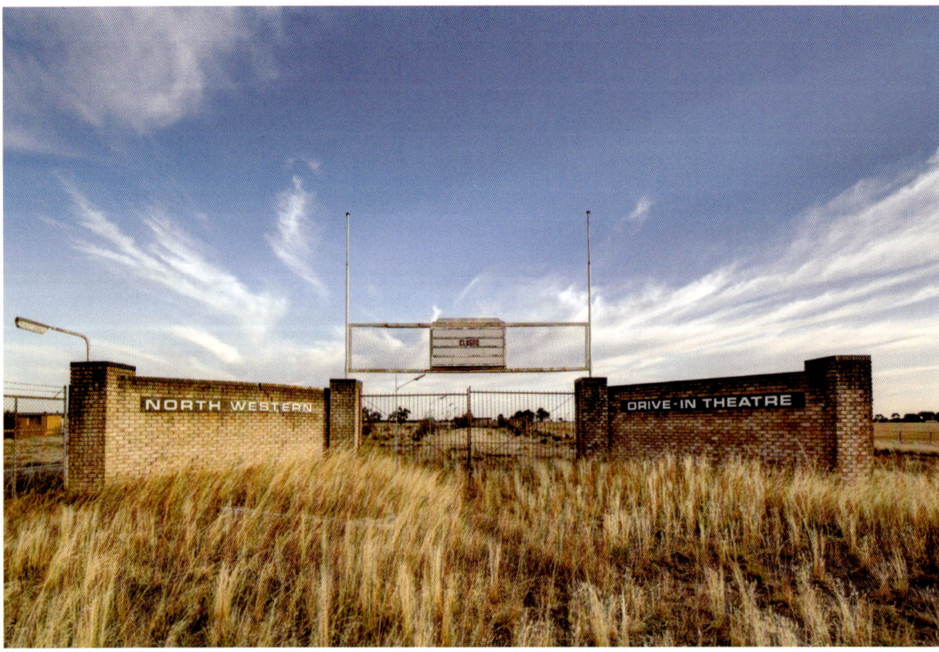

The abandoned Birchip Drive-In still bears its faded 'Closed' sign—a quiet reminder of a once-beloved gathering place that held a special spot in the heart of the community.

THE DRIVE-IN

Birchip's North-Western Drive-In was once a beloved part of the region's social landscape. Opening in the mid-1960s, it quickly became a popular destination for locals and visitors, offering an open-air cinematic experience that defined a generation. The drive-in would see long queues of cars—sometimes stretching back over a kilometre—as patrons travelled from surrounding towns such as Wycheproof, Donald and Sea Lake to enjoy a night at the movies under the stars.

Drive-in theatres played a significant role in Australian culture during the 1950s and 1960s, particularly in rural areas where entertainment options were limited. They offered a relaxed and affordable outing for families, couples and groups of friends. The Birchip Drive-In remained in operation until the mid-1980s, with 'Howard the Duck' being the last film screened before the site ceased operations. As trends shifted toward indoor multiplexes and home entertainment, the drive-in's popularity waned, leading to its permanent closure.

Today, the former site of the North-Western Drive-In is used to paddock horses and livestock, with little remaining to suggest its former purpose other than its original entranceway and signage. Yet its memory lives on in the hearts of nostalgic locals and the occasional urban explorer who visits the overgrown grounds. The site serves as a quiet monument to a bygone era of community, simplicity and shared experience, reflecting broader cultural shifts in how rural Victorians engage with entertainment—particularly in the more isolated corners of the state.

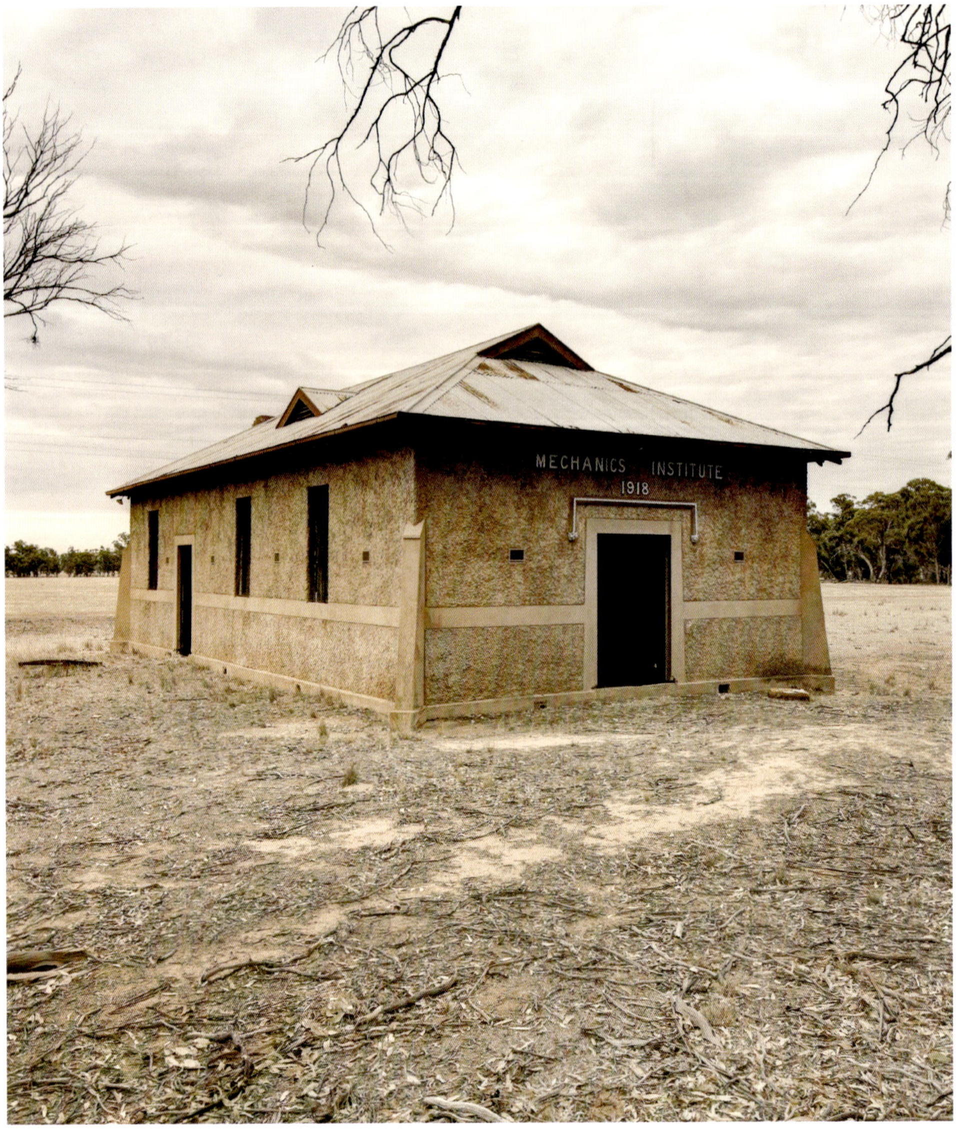

This old Mechanics Institute building in Central Victoria now serves a very different purpose—providing shelter for livestock amid its timeworn walls.

THE MECHANICS INSTITUTE

Mechanics Institutes in Australia were community hubs established in the 19th and early 20th centuries, inspired by a British movement aimed at educating the working class. They provided access to books, lectures and classes in subjects like science, literature and trades. Many evolved into public libraries, town halls or cultural centres, but some fell into disuse and abandonment as their original purpose became obsolete.

In Victoria, these institutes played a crucial role in shaping local communities, especially in rural towns. This abandoned structure located in the state's central rural district is one of many scattered across the state and reflects this broader history. It was once a gathering place for knowledge and social engagement but now stands as a relic of a bygone era. Its heritage significance lies in its representation of self-improvement, public education and the evolution of community spaces in Victoria. The buildings themselves, whether crumbling or intact, tells a story of changing societal needs and the shifting landscape of regional Australia.

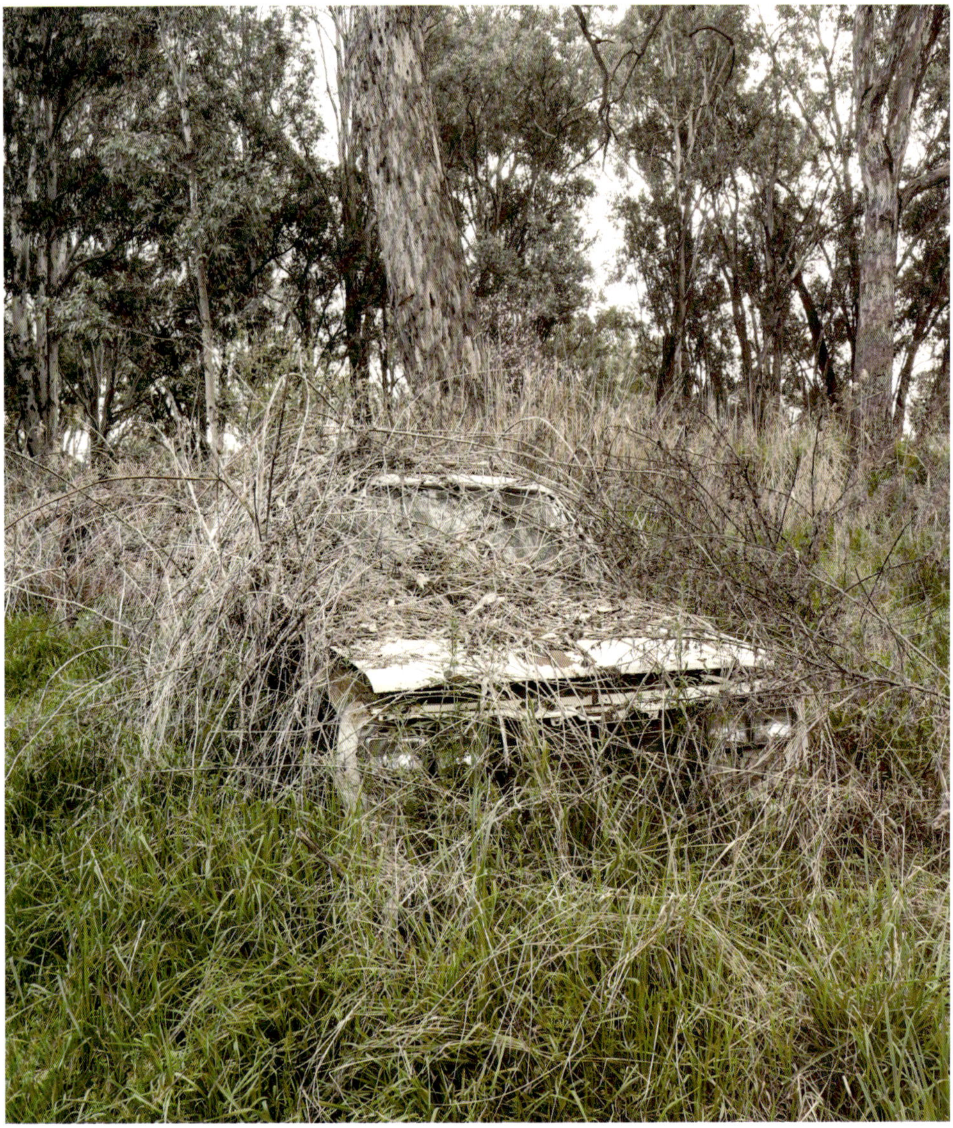

Engulfed in thick blackberry bushes, this abandoned car is nearly hidden from sight, slowly vanishing into the landscape.

CAR GRAVEYARDS

Abandoned car yards across Victoria are haunting and strangely captivating spaces. Rows of rusting vehicles sit idle beneath overgrown weeds, their windscreens cracked, paint faded and tyres deflated. Nature slowly reclaims these forgotten lots, creating a juxtaposition between industrial decay and wild regrowth. The silence that lingers in these places is almost palpable—as though the energy of countless road trips, commutes and lives in transit still hums faintly in the air. Some cars are stripped bare, scavenged for parts, while others appear eerily frozen in time, gathering dust and rain in equal measure.

These desolate spaces are more than just eerie—they reveal something fundamental about Australia's cultural connection to the car. In a country where distances are vast and public transport can be limited, especially in regional and rural areas, the car is not just a mode of transport; it is a symbol of autonomy, identity and necessity. Abandoned car yards mark the passing of that ideal; remnants of an industry once thriving but now shaped by shifting consumer habits, environmental concerns and rapid technological change.

Victoria's abandoned car yards are not the result of closed dealerships or the collapse of local manufacturing. In most cases, they are simply the product of informal accumulation—paddocks where farmers have collected old vehicles over decades, or remote plots where cars have been dumped without reason or record. Victoria, however, seems to host an unusually high number of these makeshift vehicle graveyards. While the state's once-thriving automotive industry—centred in places like Geelong, Dandenong and Broadmeadows—has left behind its own trail of obsolete machinery and shuttered operations, a separate and quieter phenomenon persists. Scattered across the countryside, small-town service yards and forgotten clearings are now home to rusting collections of vehicles from every era. These sites serve as quiet, corroded markers of economic change, environmental neglect, and Australia's evolving relationship with mobility, consumption and the impermanence of industry.

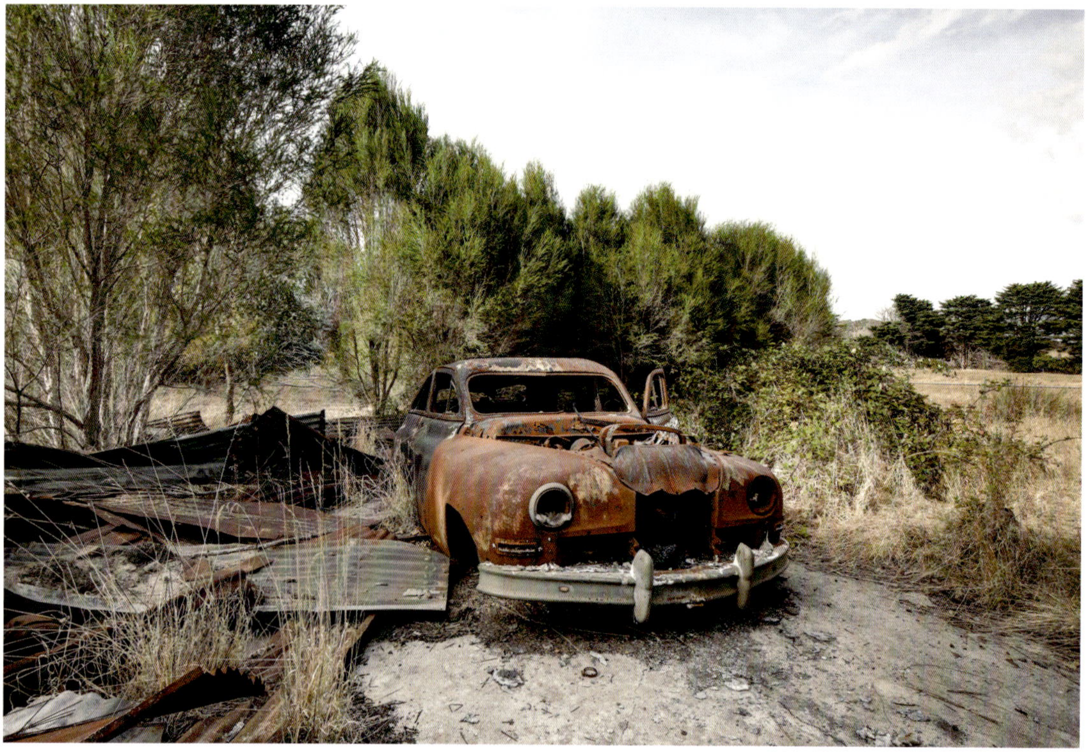

This rusted vintage car body rests quietly in a field, slowly surrendering to the passage of time.

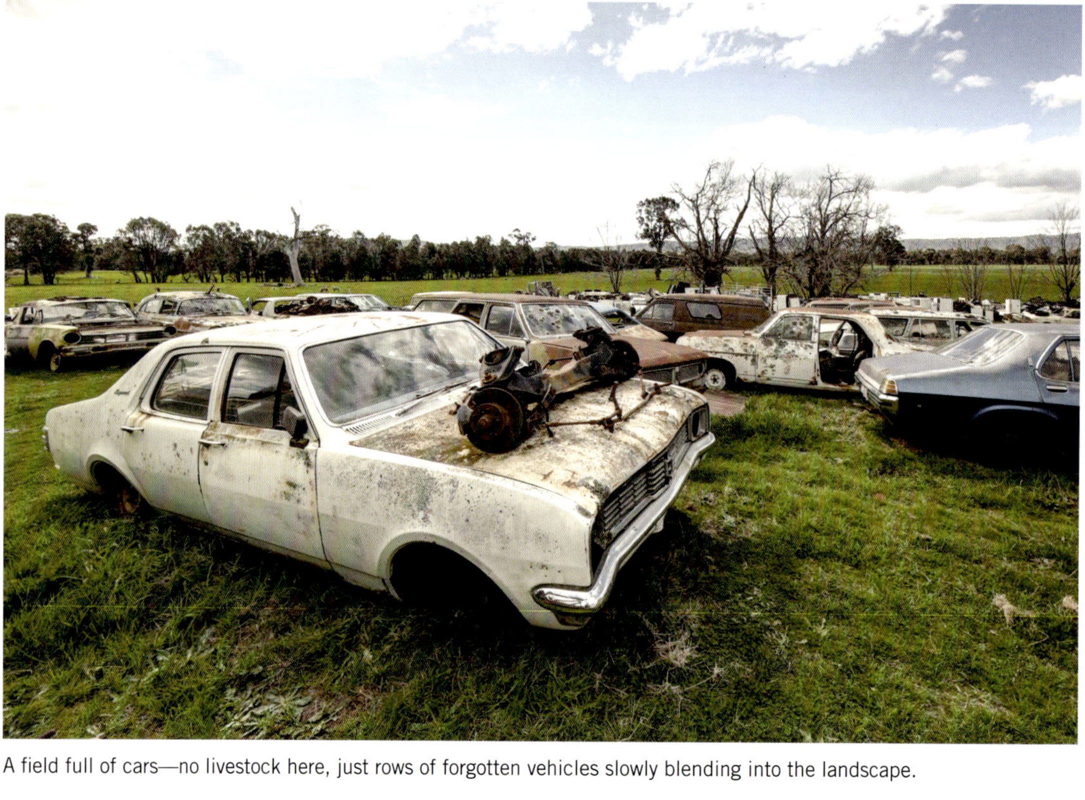

A field full of cars—no livestock here, just rows of forgotten vehicles slowly blending into the landscape.

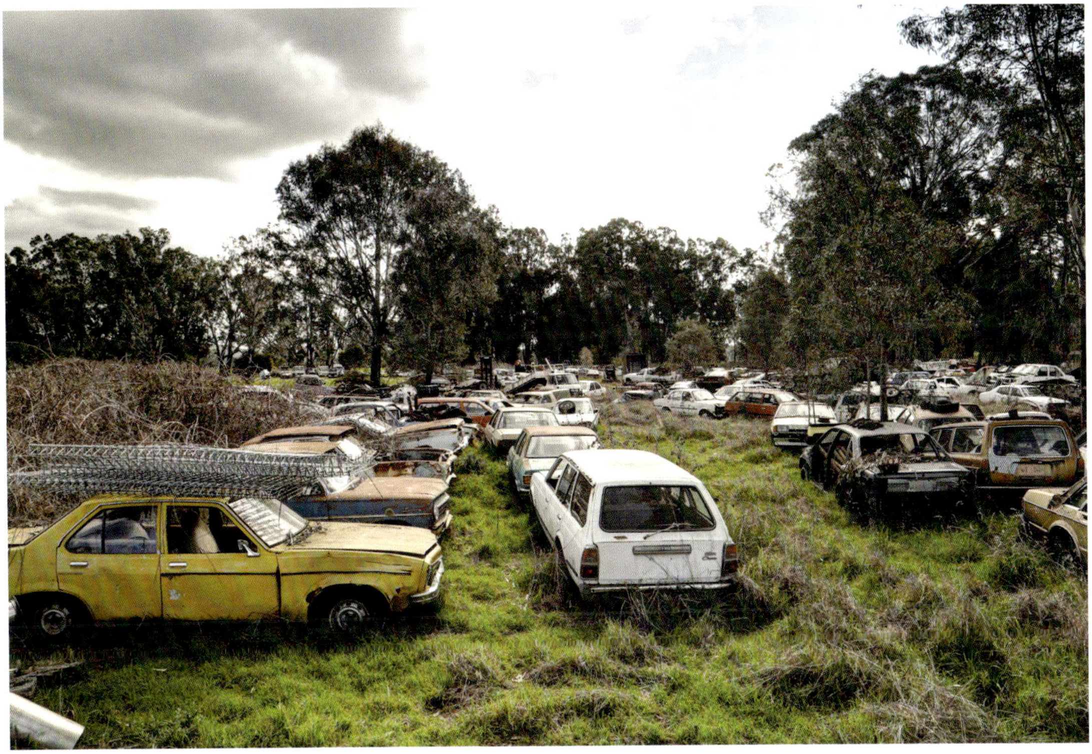

Welcome to the final resting place for these tired old rides—an automobile cemetery where engines come to take their eternal nap.

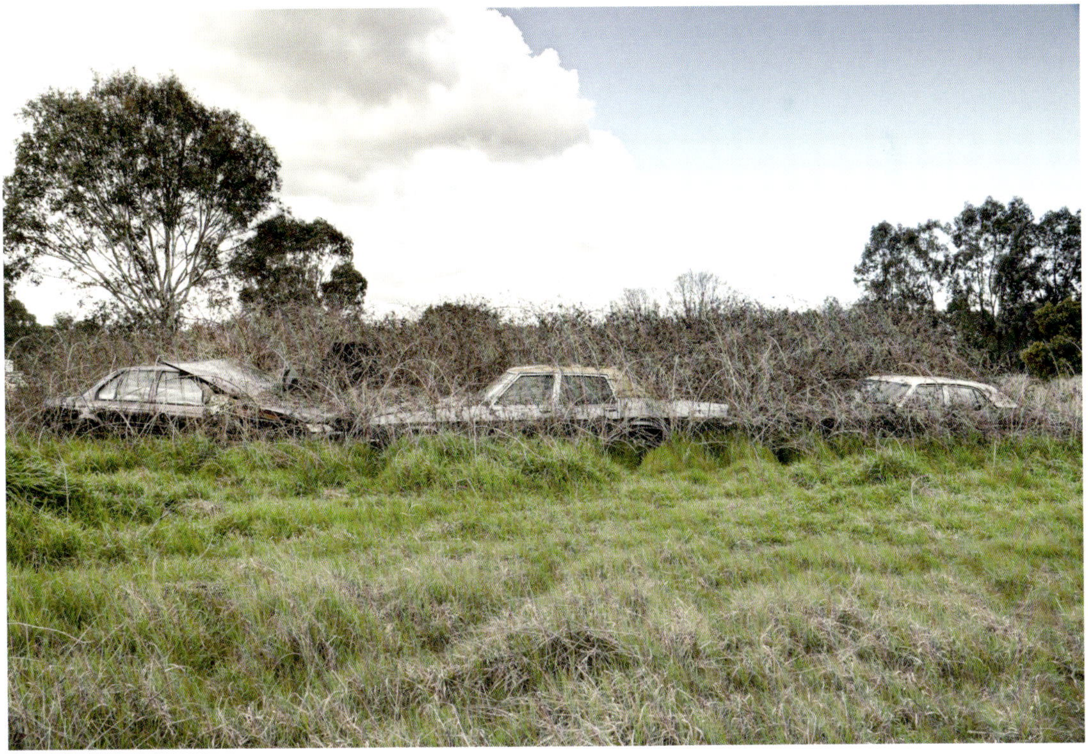

These cars are slowly being swallowed whole by nature's relentless takeover.

THE HIDDEN WORKSHOP

An abandoned workshop in Melbourne, once a bustling hub of industrial activity, now sits in quiet decay. Tucked discreetly behind frosted windows on a busy street in an inner-city suburb, the building blends into its urban surroundings, its secrets hidden in plain sight. Passers-by rarely notice the fading signage or the layers of grime that coat its facade, but within lies a haunting space frozen in time.

Inside, the walls are lined with old machinery, hand tools and industrial fittings, many of which are heavily corroded by decades of neglect. The air is thick with the scent of oil, while scattered nuts, bolts and wiring speak to a time when this space thrummed with daily activity. The workshop is not empty, though—it's now home to a flock of pigeons nesting in its upper beams—their collective coos echoing through the space. Nature, in its own way, has reclaimed the building—not with vines and trees, but with wings, feathers and faeces.

This eerie, forgotten space offers a rare glimpse into the city's industrial past, where once-vital operations supported Melbourne's booming growth. It is a surreal collision of the mechanical and the organic—steel gears beside skeletons of birds and rust next to roosts. For urban explorers and history enthusiasts, the workshop serves as a raw, un-curated museum of labour and decline. It is a poignant reminder that even in the heart of a thriving metropolis, history lingers just out of sight, waiting to be noticed through the haze of dust.

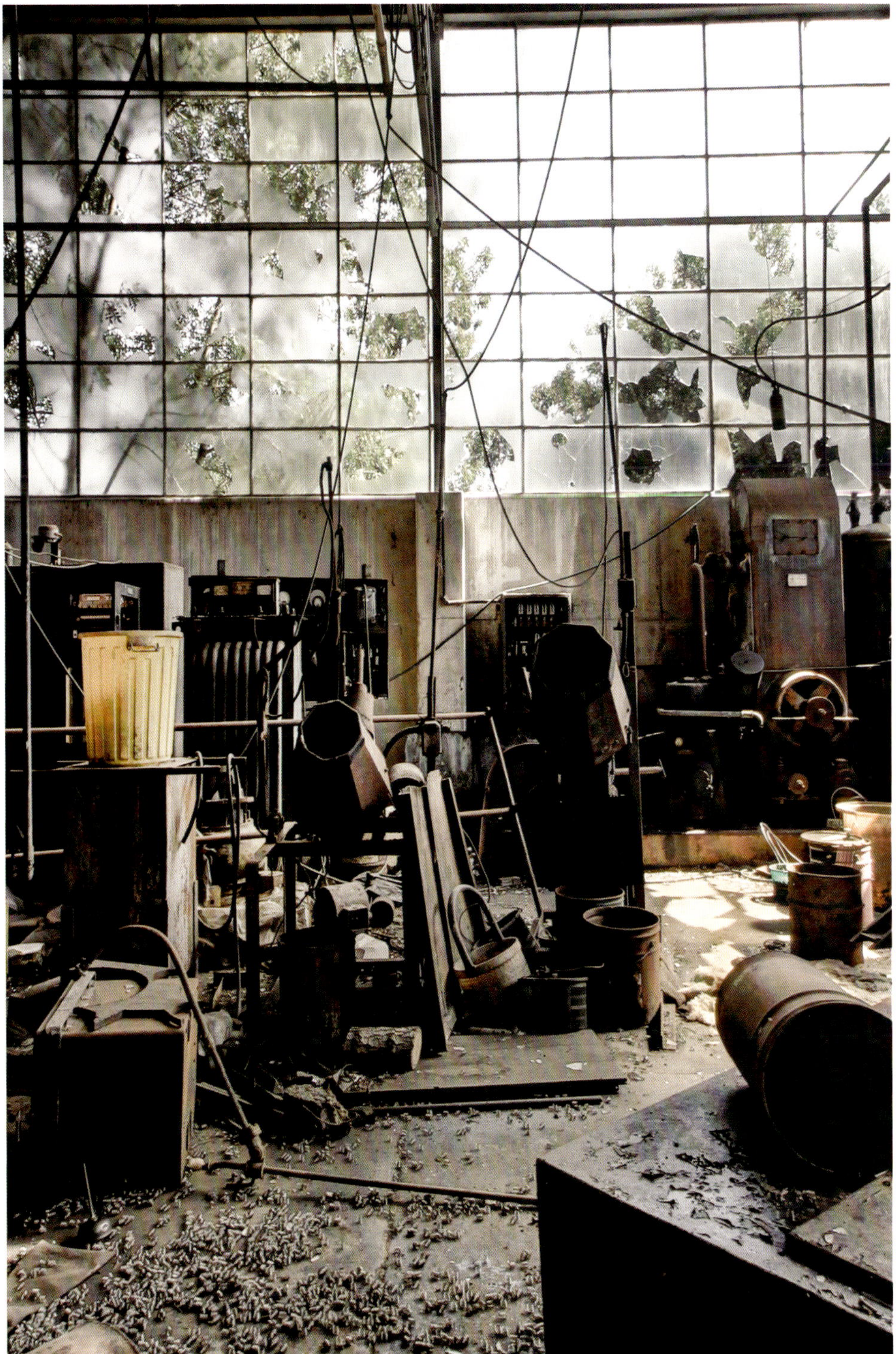

This long-forgotten workshop sat quietly beside a main road—outside, the hum of passing cars; inside, only the soft flutter of pigeons breaking the stillness.

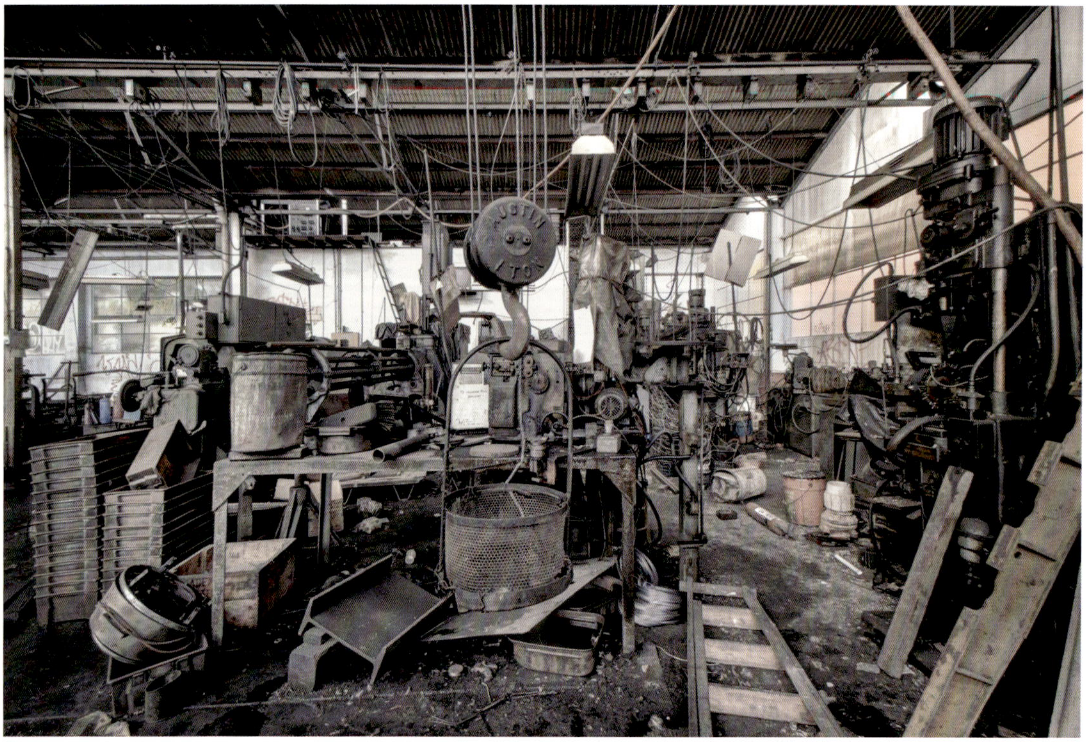

Industrial scraps lay strewn across the floors and benchtops of this abandoned workshop—rusted remnants of past labour, now silenced and slowly succumbing to time.

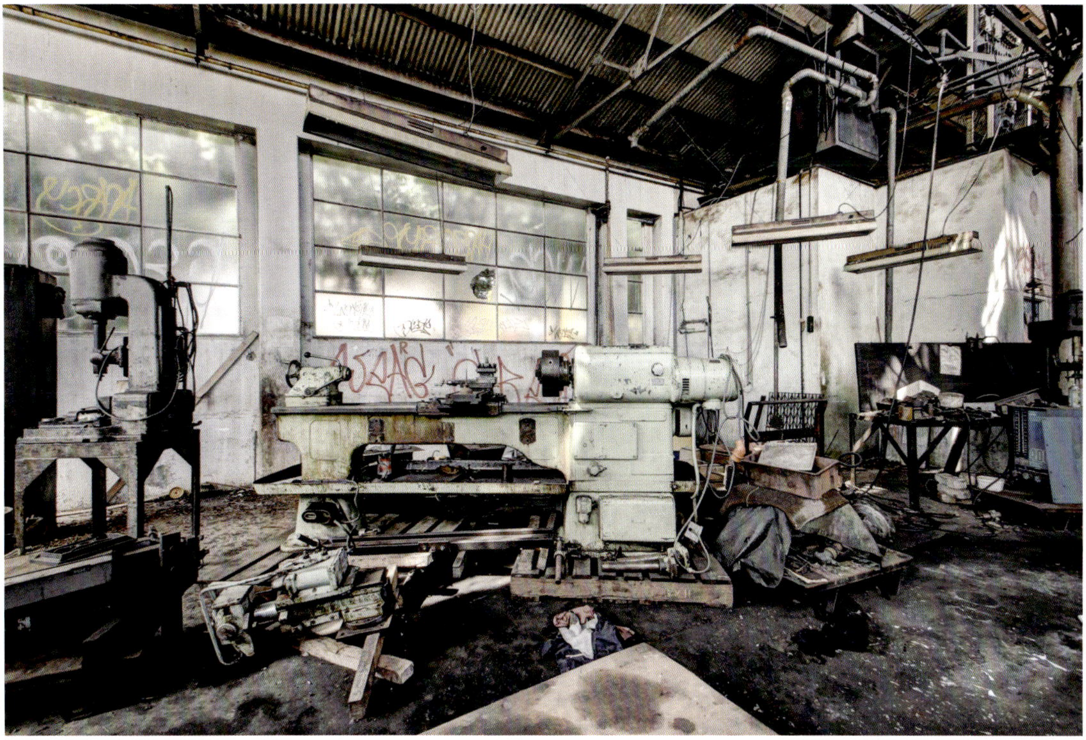

Industrial lights hang above the former workshop like ghosts, casting dim shadows over a graveyard of lifeless machinery and forgotten tools.

CALDER PARK RACEWAY

Calder Park Raceway, on the outskirts of Melbourne, was once one of Australia's most recognised motorsport venues. Opening in the early 1960s, it played host to an eclectic range of events—from drag racing and touring car championships to lesser-known local competitions. Its most distinctive feature, the 'Thunderdome', a steeply banked oval track built in the late 1980s, was a bold and ambitious addition that briefly drew international attention.

But Calder Park wasn't just about racing. In the early 1990s, it briefly became a massive concert venue. In 1993, Guns N' Roses played at the raceway as part of their 'Use Your Illusion' world tour. The event drew an estimated 75,000 people—one of the largest crowds the venue ever hosted. It was loud, chaotic and unforgettable, with stories still circulating about the dust, traffic jams and sheer scale of the night. The concert added a layer of cultural mythology to a space already rich in motor-racing lore.

Over time, however, the site became a victim of shifting trends. By the early 2000s, activity had slowed considerably, with only sporadic events keeping the venue partially alive. Parts of the raceway fell into disuse and maintenance dwindled. Today, much of Calder Park sits in limbo—neither fully active nor completely abandoned. Grandstands crumble, advertising banners fade under the sun and long-forgotten trackside structures stand rusting among the weeds.

For urban explorers and photographers, the site offers a rich visual experience. Nature is slowly reclaiming the edges—invasive scotch thistle sprouts through cracked asphalt, vines creep up shattered fences and wind whistles through empty service buildings. The contrast between the site's high-octane past and its quiet, overgrown present is striking. Every rusted gate and peeling sign seems to echo the roar of engines and crowds. Though its future remains uncertain, Calder Park endures as a bittersweet monument to the rise, reinvention and quiet decline of a once-thriving motorsport and cultural venue.

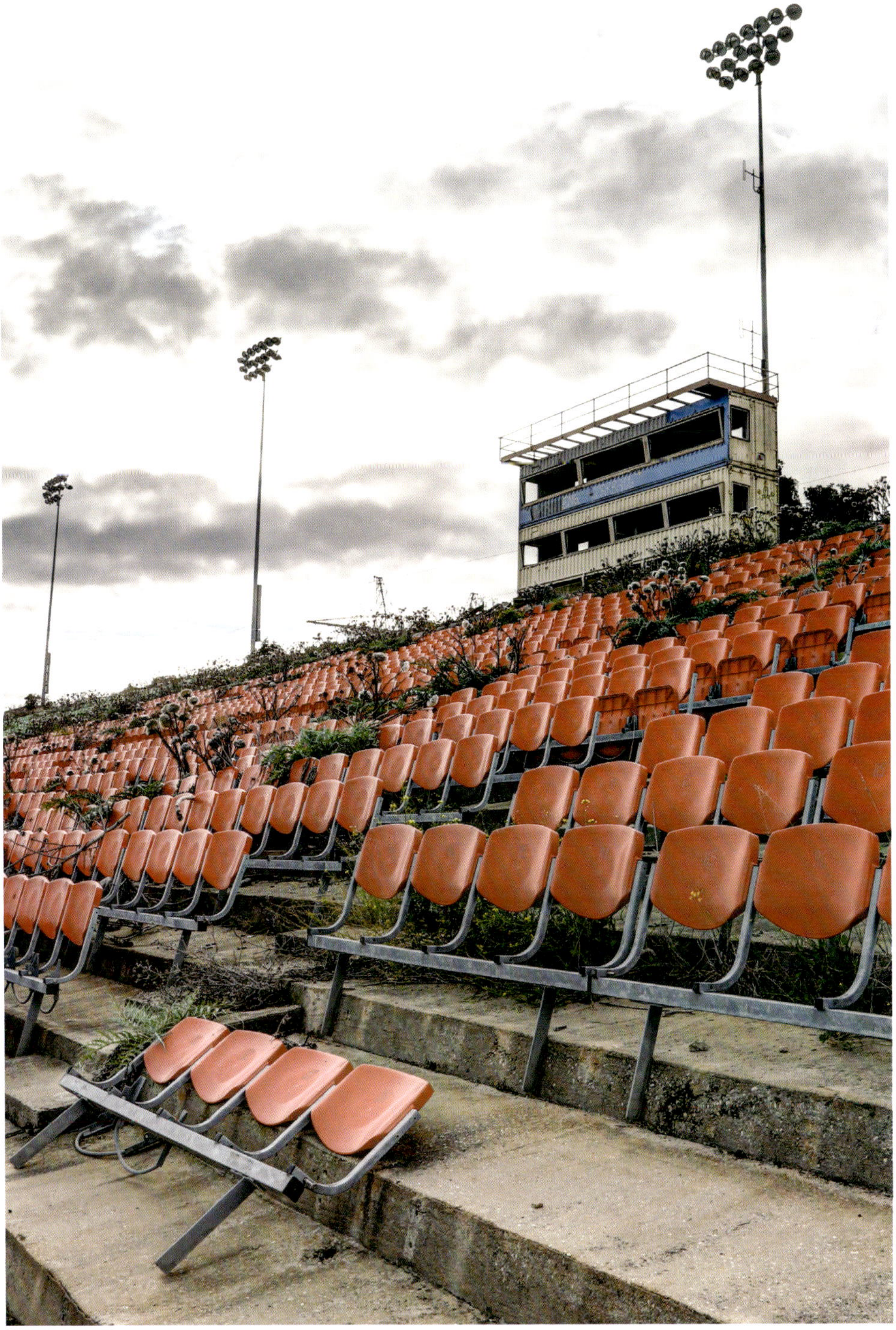

Red seats at the derelict Calder Park Raceway sit empty under the open sky—the only spectators now are the encroaching scotch thistles, reclaiming the stands one thorn at a time.

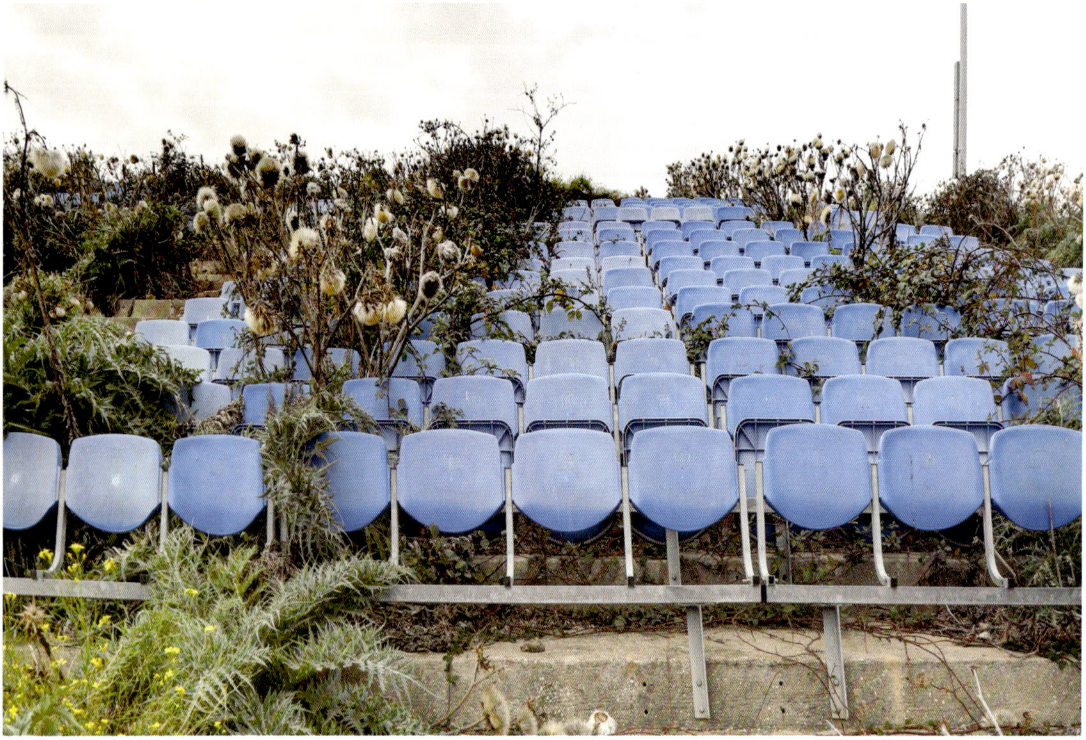

These fading blue seats once held rows of eager spectators—now they sit silent and weathered, watching over memories that have long since faded.

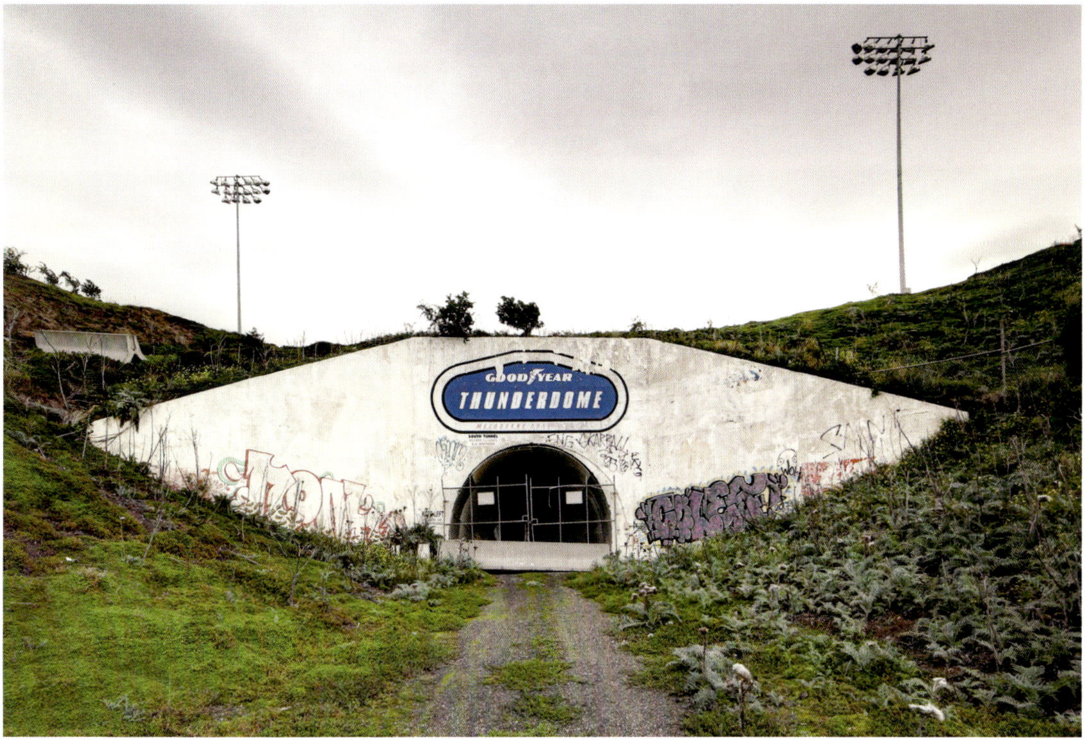

The grim entrance to the racetrack stands weathered and unwelcoming—a fading gateway to a place once charged with speed, noise and adrenaline, now surrendered to silence and decay.

SWIMMING POOLS

The abandoned swimming pools scattered across Victoria hold a unique place in the state's social and recreational history. Many of these pools were once thriving community hubs during a time of suburban expansion and growing interest in public leisure. Often nestled within local parks or attached to sports clubs, they provided a popular gathering place for families and children during the warmer months, offering relief from the heat and a strong sense of community.

However, as time passed, changing demographics, rising maintenance costs and shifting leisure preferences contributed to the slow decline of many of these facilities. Some were replaced by more modern and much larger aquatic centres, while others simply fell into disrepair—quietly overtaken by weeds, cracked concrete and the slow erosion of time.

Today, urban explorers and photographers are drawn to their silent, empty basins and crumbling edges—spaces once filled with noise, laughter and movement now rendered still and stark. In recent years, street artists have also reclaimed these empty shells, transforming their concrete surfaces into vibrant canvases where new forms of expression emerge from forgotten spaces.

These sites offer a visual narrative of changing times, capturing the quiet moment between public memory and forgotten infrastructure. In their decay, Victoria's abandoned pools remain deeply symbolic of community, climate and the impermanence of shared spaces.

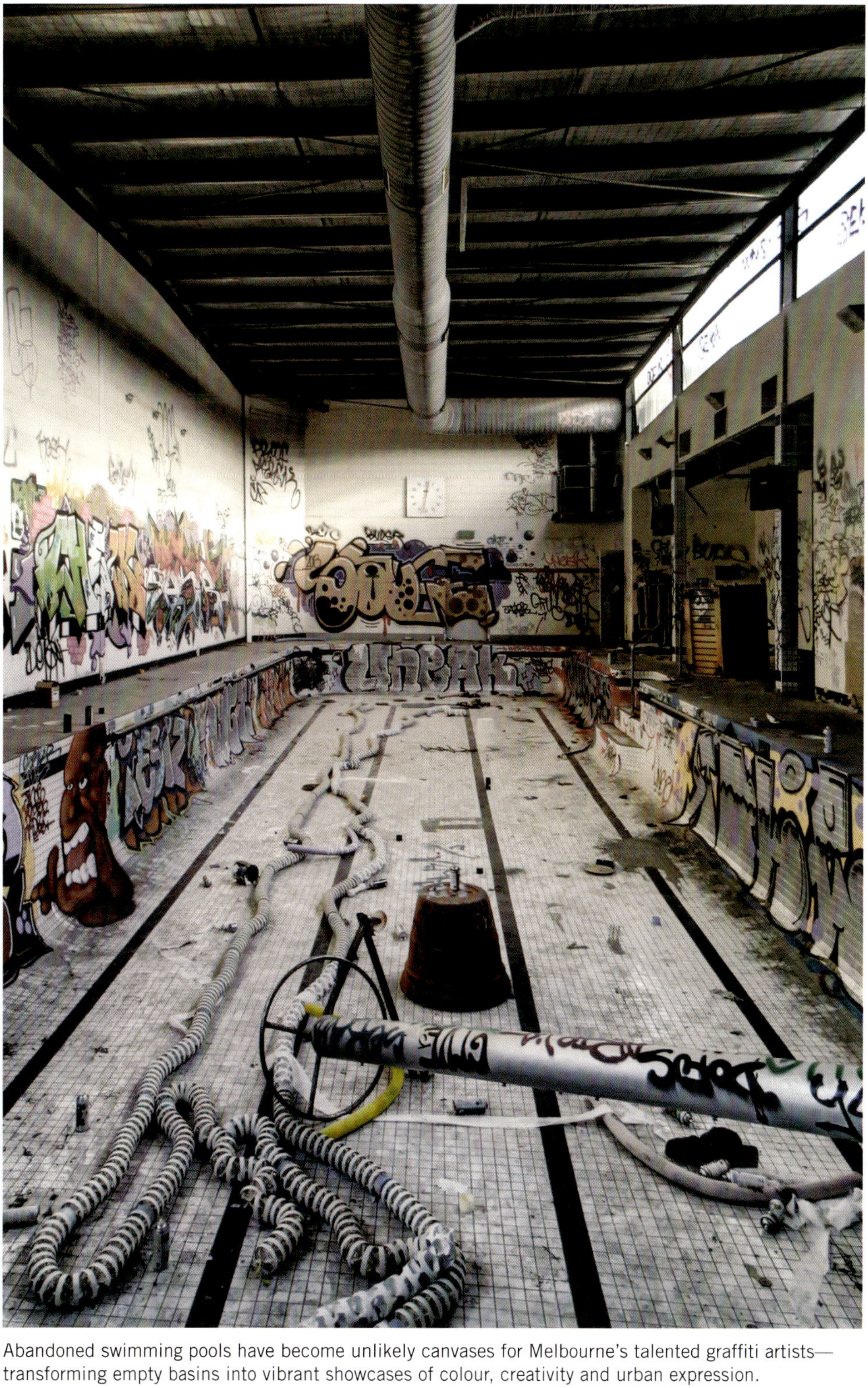

Abandoned swimming pools have become unlikely canvases for Melbourne's talented graffiti artists—transforming empty basins into vibrant showcases of colour, creativity and urban expression.

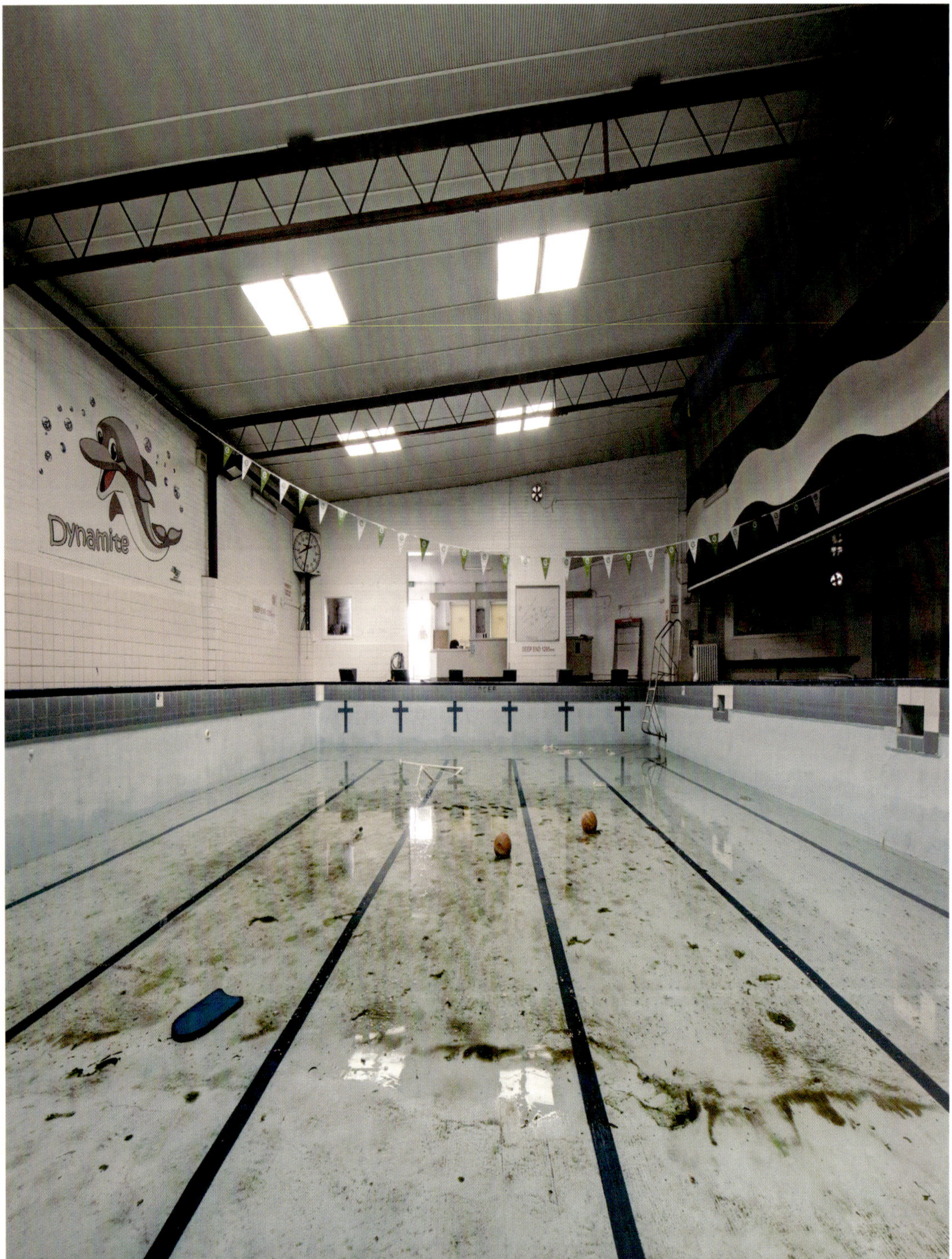

This abandoned swimming pool in Melbourne's inner suburbs now sits lifeless and empty—a hollow shell that once echoed with the sounds of splashes and laughter, now silent beneath layers of dust.

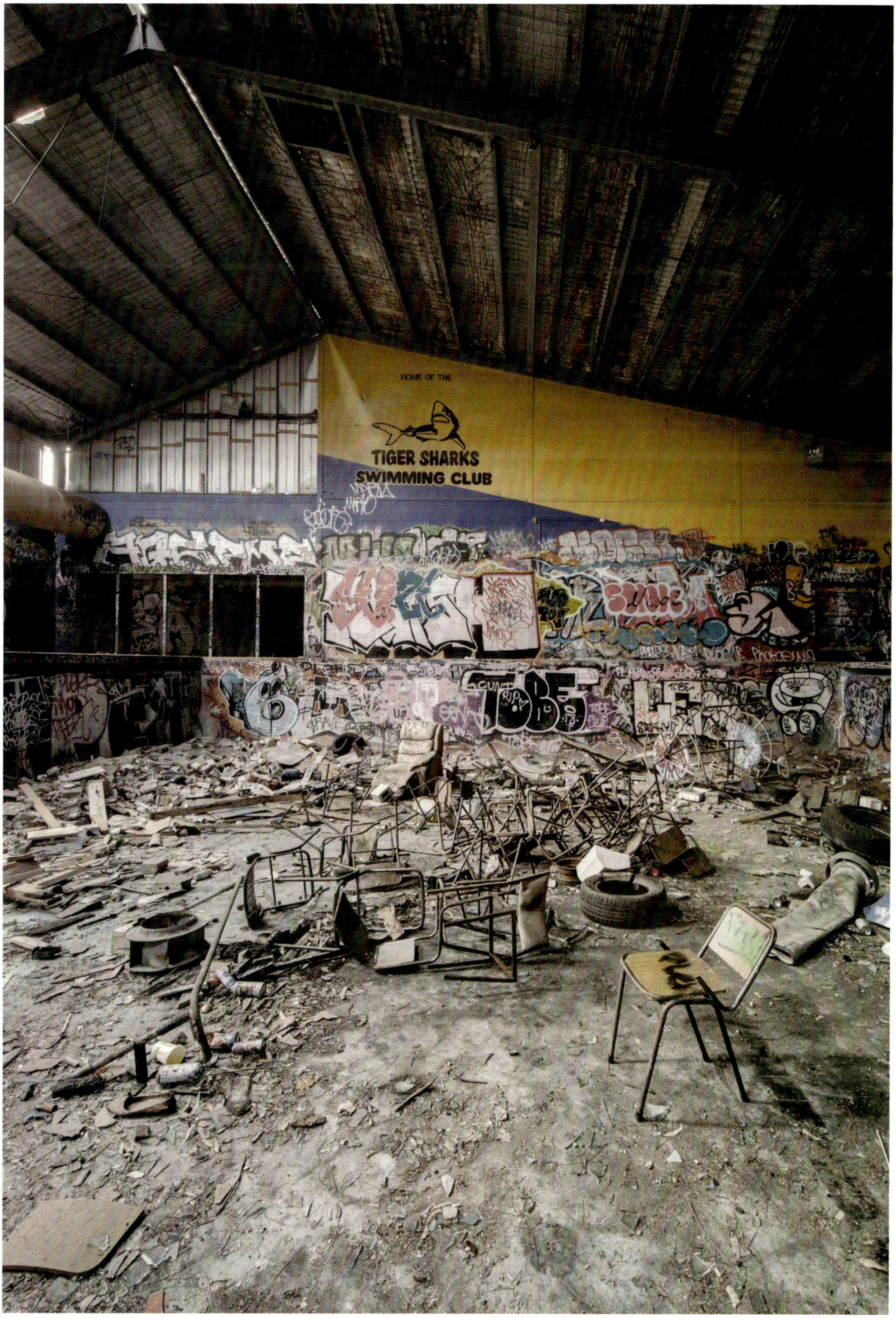

The only thing drowning in this long-abandoned pool are the layers of graffiti—vivid, chaotic, and ever-growing.

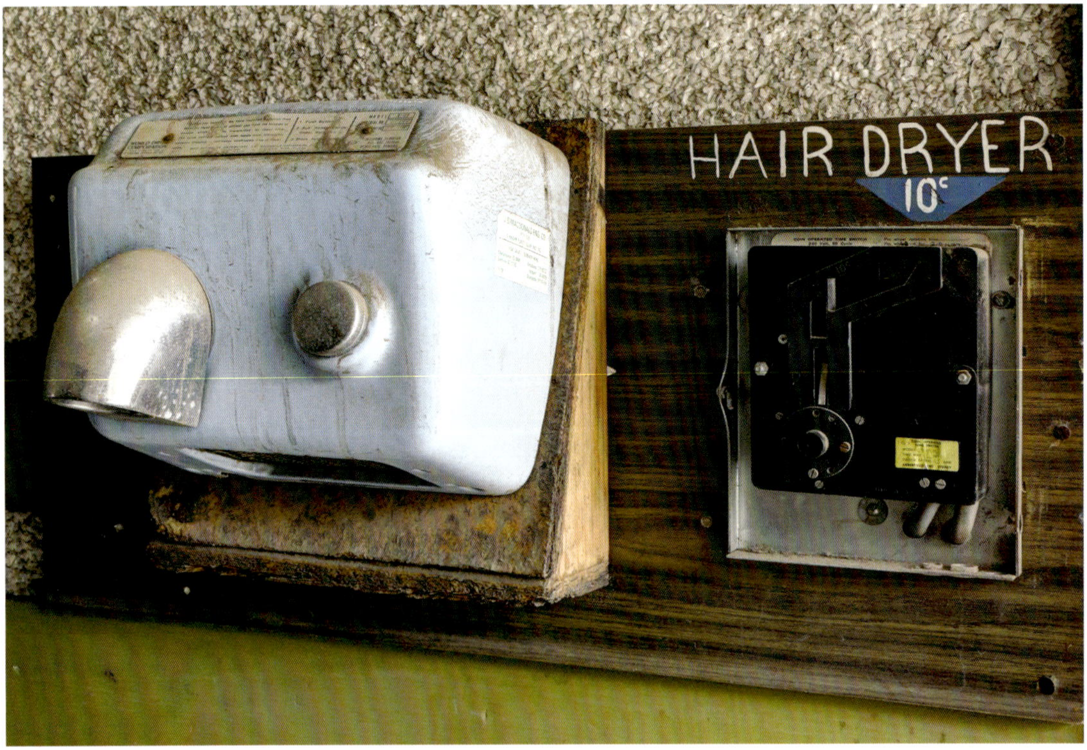

This vintage hairdryer, mounted on the change room wall, once offered swimmers a warm blast of air for just 10 cents—a small comfort in a bygone era of public pools.

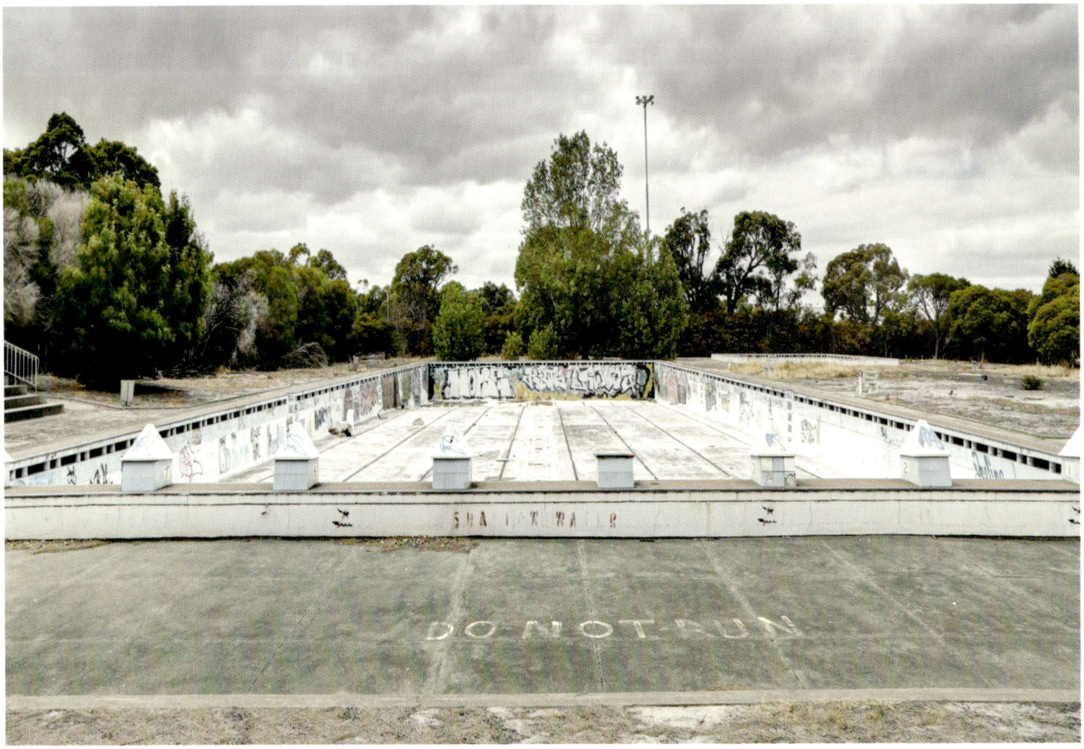

A multi-lane swimming pool now sits empty—its once-busy lanes dry and cracked, echoing with memories of races, splashes, and summer afternoons long past.

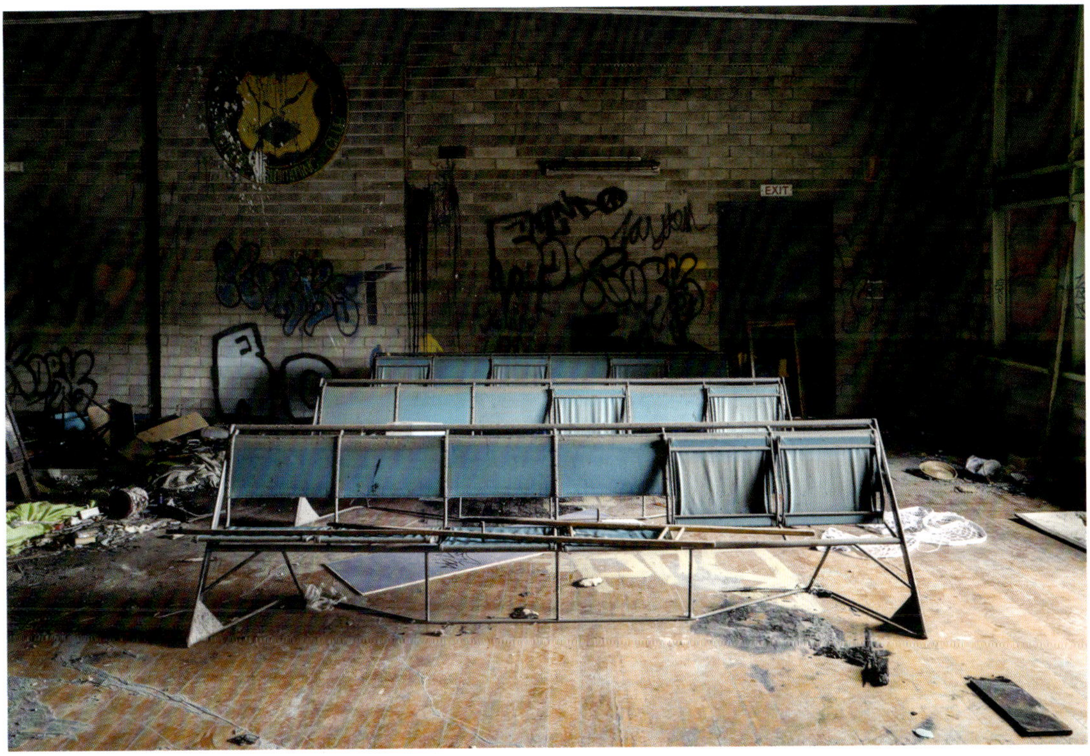

The swim team's old clubroom still held a few relics from the past—faded banners and scattered memorabilia quietly echoing a time of community and competition.

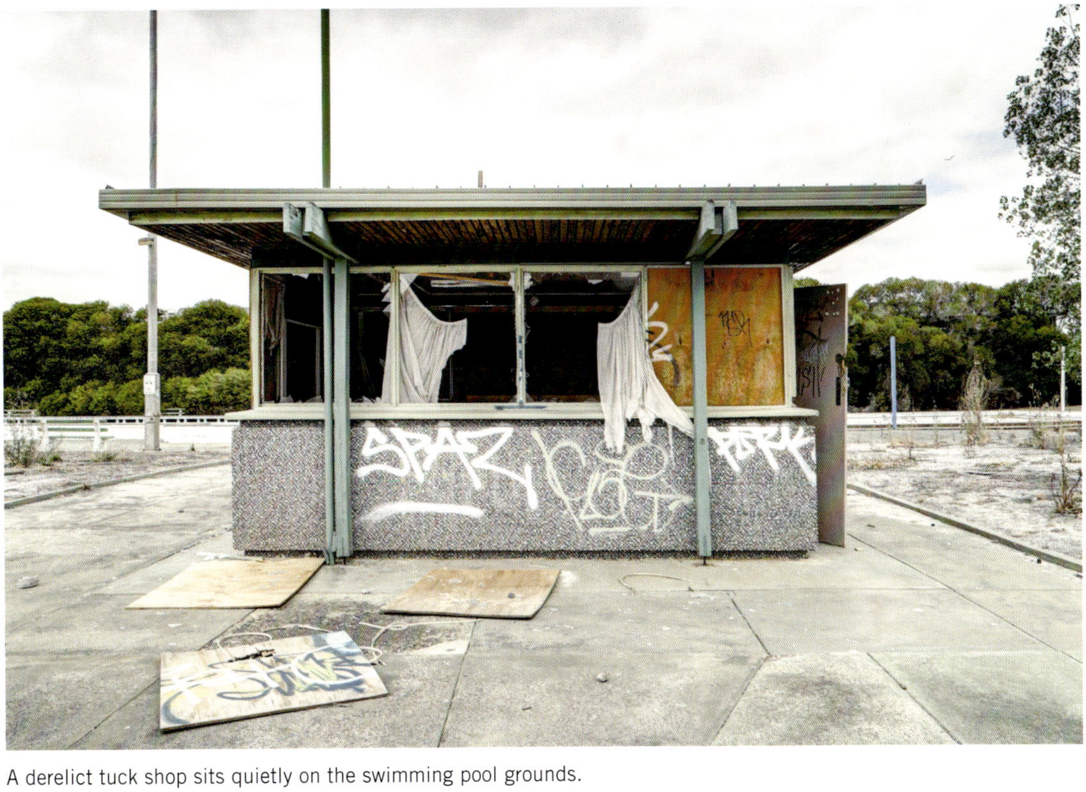

A derelict tuck shop sits quietly on the swimming pool grounds.

COUNTRY CHAPELS

Abandoned country chapels across Victoria are poignant symbols of the state's religious and cultural history. Built mostly in the 19th and early 20th centuries, these chapels served rural communities, providing a space for worship, gatherings and important life events such as baptisms, weddings and funerals. Many were constructed during periods of early settlement, often funded by local families or church congregations, and became central to the social and spiritual lives of isolated communities.

As rural populations shifted and agricultural practices changed, many of these chapels faced declining congregations and were eventually abandoned. The structures, often modest in design, now represent the material traces of shifting social landscapes, with some falling into disrepair due to lack of maintenance as the community moved on.

Today, abandoned country chapels serve as important historical landmarks, reflecting Victoria's early settlement patterns, religious practices and the social dynamics of rural life. Their decaying interiors and silent exteriors offer a quiet reminder of the changing landscape of faith, community and the passage of time in the state's rural areas.

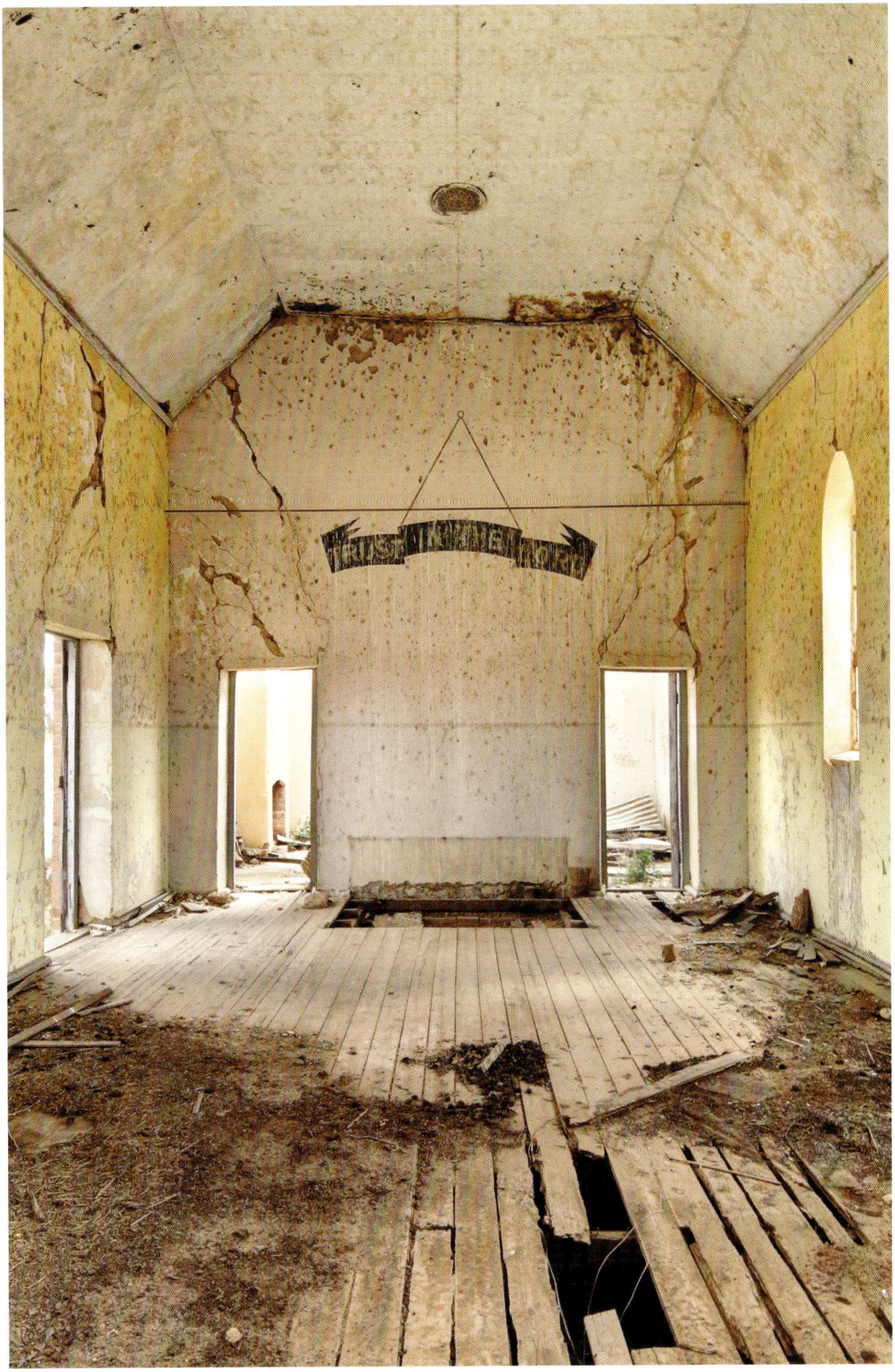

'Trust In The Lord' is faintly scrawled on a weathered banner inside this long-abandoned church in Victoria's northwest.

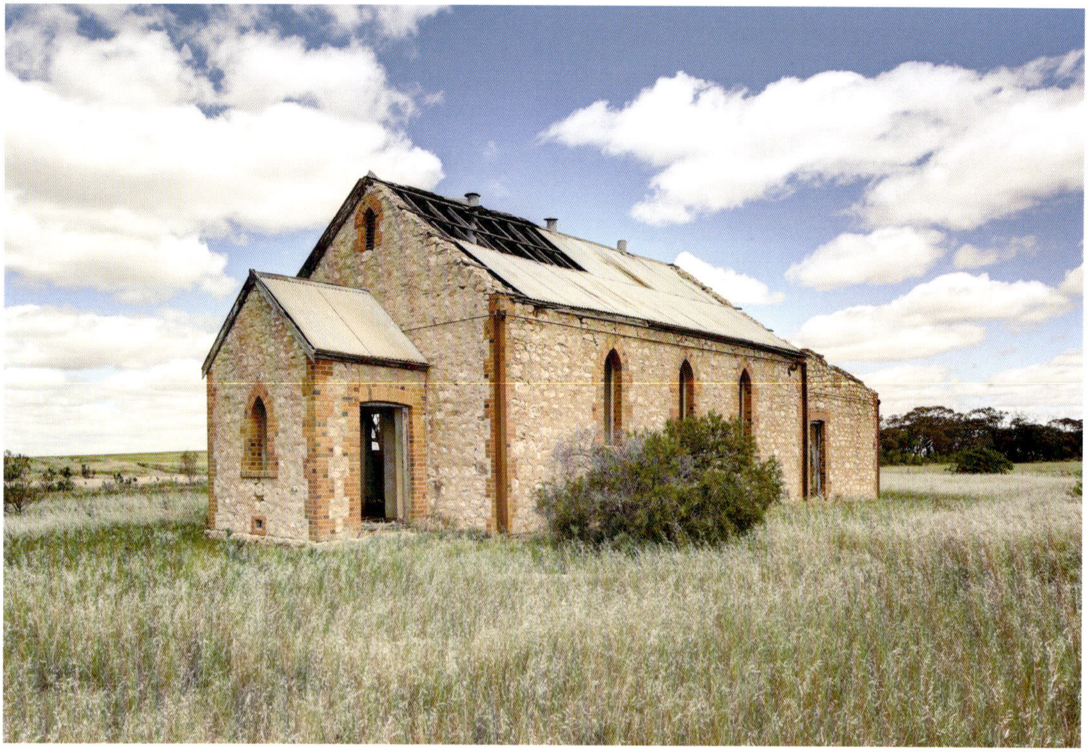

This long-abandoned church shows signs of decay, with its roof beginning to crumble.

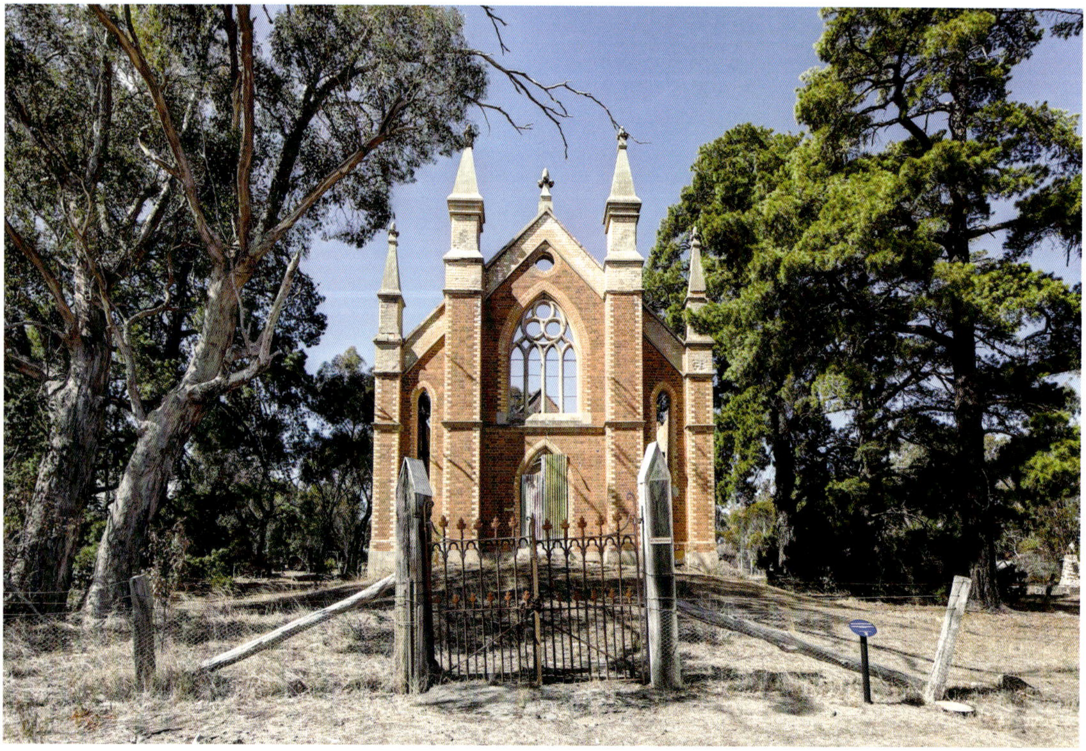

The skeletal shell of an abandoned church stands silent in the heart of the state, its weathered frame whispering stories long forgotten.

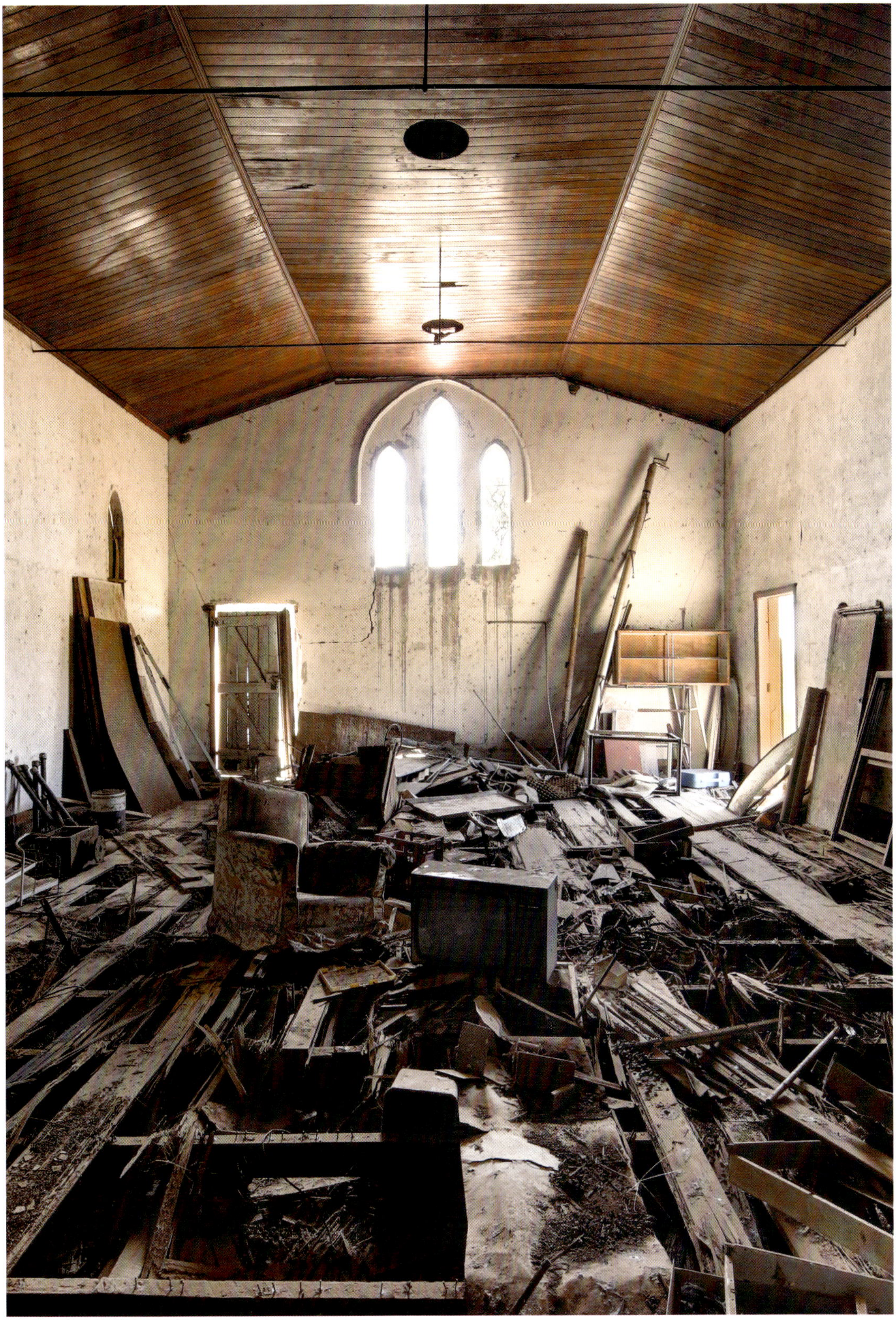

The interior of this abandoned church was strewn with upended floorboards and scattered with the remnants of people's lives—a forgotten sanctum barely holding the traces of those who once prayed here.

ALSO FROM WOODSLANE PRESS

The *Australia Through Time* books are published by Woodslane Press. The imprint is best known for Australia's bestselling series of walking guides, available via woodslanepress.com.au. If your local bookshop does not have stock of a Woodslane Press book, they can easily order it for you. In case of difficulty please contact our customer service team on 02 8445 2300 or info@woodslane.com.au.

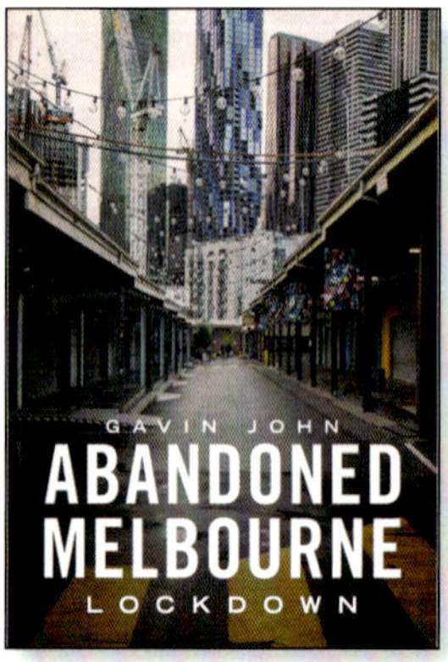

Abandoned Melbourne
$24.99
ISBN: 9781925868715

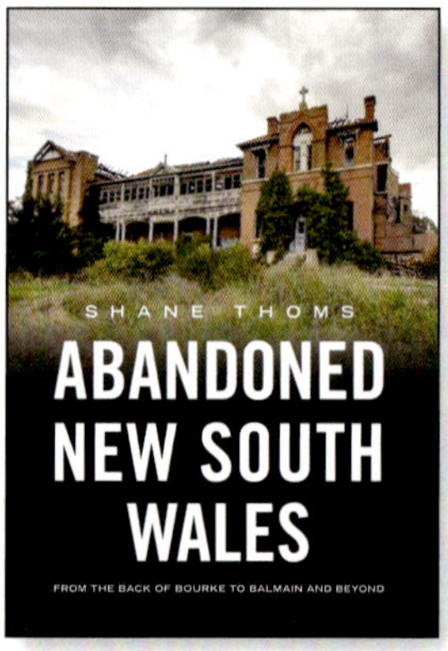

Abandoned
New South Wales
$24.99
ISBN: 9781922800473

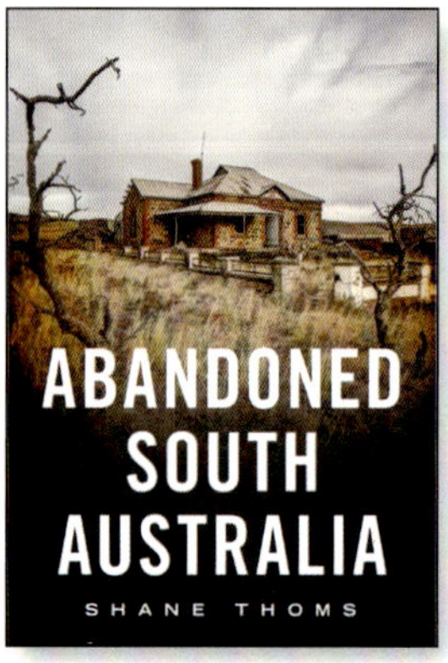

Abandoned
South Australia
$24.99
ISBN: 9781925868913

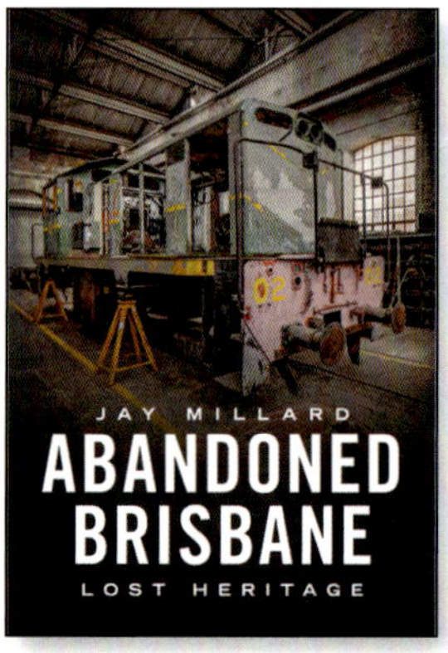

Abandoned Brisbane
$24.99
ISBN: 9781925868722